What Do You Have?

The Secret of Experiencing Exponential Growth and Productivity

Eric Tangumonkem, Ph.D.

IEM PRESS

PO Box 831001, Richardson, TX 75080
A Subsidiary of IEM APPROACH

ISBN 13: 978-1-63603-004-3

Library of Congress Catalog Card Number: 2020943936

Table of Contents

Dedication

To our children, Afaamboma, Ntsongmboma, Elotmboma, Abeutmboma, and Atesamboma, who, during one of the low points of our lives, used an empty shoebox to remind me of what is important.

Introduction

What do you have? When asked, many people will respond that they have nothing. Those who say they have nothing may be saying this because they want other people to feel sympathetic toward them. Others think it is a sign of humility to be modest about how you talk in terms of what you have. When asked this question in the midst of a difficult situation, how you respond determines if you will be successful in overcoming whatever challenge you are facing.

When you find any principle in the Bible repeated both in the Old and the New Testament, it is crucial to pay close attention to it. There are two instances, both in the Old and the New Testament, in which different people under different circumstances were asked the following question: "What do you have?"

This book examines the circumstances under which this question was asked, as well as the outcome. Then we can apply the lessons learned to our lives today; we are all facing challenges and need to learn the secret for stepping into unlimited growth and reaching our full potential.

While there are countless theories as to why many people are poor, never reaching their personal best, many of these theories and explanations fail to factor in what people already have. Most proposed solutions are focused on the externals, but here, we will be focusing on what you *already have*.

This will be a subtle yet profound change, unleashing unlimited growth and productivity in your life. Those around you will not even recognize who you are! While many people are distracted or discouraged by what is happening in the lives of others, perhaps feeling abandoned or rejected, you will be empowered. You will learn how to use the tools and resources you already have to live the life you have always desired and deserve.

The first chapter focuses on why I wrote this book. It dwells on my personal story and how the message in this book has had a profound impact on my life – and how it can change your life.

Chapter two challenges you to stop complaining; that's your worst internal enemy. You will meet Moses, who tried to whine his way out of an important assignment God had given him, but God would not let Moses off the hook. When you complain, you have lost control of your circumstances, incapacitating and preventing you from reaching your full potential. Why do people think complaining will bring solutions to their problems? The truth is that complaining and living in despair sucks the energy out of you, digging a deeper hole than the hole you're already in! You cannot complain your way to a solution; therefore, you must stop complaining and start conquering. You do not need sympathy and self-pity; they will keep you grounded and prevent you from stepping into the best that God has for you.

Chapter three deals with how to see and understand what you *already have*. The emphasis is not on what other people have, because you are unique and different from them. There is no point in trying to be like other people; you already have all that you need to become you and fulfill your purpose. You must not compare yourself to others, especially when you so in a negative sense. We will expand on this and show why it is more profitable to know what you already have; each of us already has what we need to accomplish our purpose in life.

In chapter four, we'll look at the issue of bad things happening in our lives. We all understand that bad things happen to good people; this is true for all people! The issue is not that difficult situations occur, but how we handle those things when they come along. You'll learn that no matter what takes place, you already have what you need to face it, being bold, confident, and courageous as you think about the present and the future.

Chapter five tackles another question that many people ask during difficulties or calamity: "Why me?" They aren't thinking about what they have when experiencing problems or when some calamity befalls them; that's the wrong question. Instead, consider, "If not me, who else?" When you embrace the truth that *you have all that is needed* to go through the upcoming challenge, you will operate out of boldness, peace, and confidence – not fear.

Chapter six, the high point of this book, deals with the secret of unleashing unlimited productivity and accomplishment. You will seldom meet a person who does not want to prosper and thrive; yet, many people are struggling to succeed because they are approaching "success" incorrectly. In this chapter, you will be shown how to unleash the success that is already built into you.

It does not matter where you are in your journey –you'll discover something in this book that will help you move to the next level. I only ask that you have an open mind and investigate what I am writing before you reject it. There is nothing more powerful than knowing what you have and using it. When I say "knowing," I'm not referring to *head knowledge*, because many people **know** about many things that are not true. Other people say they know, but the truth must transform their lives or change their actions.

The question "What do you have?" will be a recurring theme throughout the entire book. Upon finishing, you'll recognize that you are already whole and complete – nothing can be added from the outside to make you any better. You must learn how to grow in awareness from the inside-out, understanding what you have, and making use of it. Embracing truth involves acting upon it. Do you know what you have? Are you using it?

CHAPTER ONE

Why I Wrote This Book

My wife made me write this book; there is no other explanation. She has been relaying the impact this message had on her life the first time she heard me deliver it, and the impact *it continues to have*. Over the years, her desire had been for me to share that message with a broader audience, and now, after more than twenty years, I believe it is time.

A lot has transpired since I preached on this topic in a small rural church on the outskirts of Buea, Cameroon. I was a second-year student at the University of Buea, and already engaged to my wife, when I went to the church to preach on the topic, "What do you have?"

Little did I know that my fiancée – now my wife – was listening to the message intently and that it had a profound impact on her. Now that we are married, sometimes the lessons in the message will come up, and she reminds me of how strongly it brought things into perspective for her. Finally, it's time to share the message with a broader audience and present a more in-depth version. It has been over twenty years since that night in Buea, and I've witnessed firsthand the power of knowing what you have and making use of it.

Leave Your Job

In 2016, the oil and gas industry went through one of its all-too-frequent downturns. During these slumps, driven by low prices, hundreds (if not thousands) of workers are laid off. This one was so severe that close to half-a-million people in the industry lost their jobs; I was one of them.

My wife secured a position at the university from which she had just graduated, but after one month, she came home and told me that she was leaving the job. My first reaction was, "You must be kidding!" Here I was, unemployed, and she was talking about *quitting her job!* How would we pay our mortgage, feed our five children, and take care of other pressing needs? Despite this obvious challenge, I could not insist that she keep working when she felt she was being led in another direction.

The way forward was not an easy one. Our youngest son was a little over a year old and needed someone to look after him. Until then, none of our children had been placed in daycare; we had decided that we didn't want them looked after by other people. Our main reason for this was that we wanted to instill our family values in our children while they were still young, so they would be successful as they grew older. During the one month that my wife was working, I took care of our son, but now, she would stay at home while I tried to figure out what to do.

I felt it was time for me to leave the oil and gas industry, transitioning to something else. Clearly, we wouldn't have an immediate income. Therefore, the financial pressure on us was immense; we had just bought a house hoping that my job in that industry would help pay the mortgage. Now that the job was gone, we didn't have enough money to pay our monthly bills, much less the mortgage.

That was when my wife started thinking about the message again: "What do you have?" After twenty years, its impact was still evident. She started praying and thinking, assessing what she had at hand, and considering how she could use it in our present situation.

After much time in prayer and contemplation, she realized that she already had the following:

- a master's degree in child development
- a great deal of experience taking care of children, both in clinical settings and with her own
- a house in a safe neighborhood

Bingo! She connected the dots and decided that she would start a home daycare.

Her reasons were twofold. First, she could take care of our son at home. Second, she would be paid for taking care of other children as well. She put in the paperwork and got the necessary permits to launch her idea.

After three months of waiting, she had registered her first child, and with time, she was able to operate at full capacity. She was now taking care of our young son and being paid for it; she made more money than she had earned at the university! Besides running the home daycare, she was inspired to open her own practice as a parenting consultant – even more rewarding professionally, emotionally, and financially.

Now, two years after quitting her university job, my wife is so excited because things are getting better and better for her. She believes that the decision to change paths was the best answer – and I agree with her.

I have personally witnessed what happens when you make use of what you already have at hand; the benefits are always easy to see in hindsight. The day my wife came home and told me she was going to stop working, I didn't like it because my focus was on what we were going through and what we would lose. I didn't think about what might be gained in the process; I wasn't even thinking about that as a possibility. Now, however, I agree that it was the best decision – and one of the best things that ever happened to us.

There is no substitute for discovering what you already have and deploying it to resolve whatever issue or challenge you are facing. The natural reaction for most people is to look for help and resources from somewhere else. That makes sense because, when encountering an obstacle, the last thing on your mind is what it will take to resolve the issue. It is naturally more comforting when you expect that help will come from somewhere else; it removes your responsibility for solving the problem.

Most people are afraid to be in charge because when things go wrong, they do not want the blame. This explains why they tend to look for solutions from other people and other sources (not that there is something wrong with looking for an answer or asking for help from other people.) There are a place and time to ask for help in seeking solutions, but here, we are focusing on how you identify and make use of what you already have.

Fortunately, most of what some consider insurmountable obstacles can be easily overcome, but they must identify that they already have what is needed to get them through. That is why this book was written – to highlight the potential *already in you* and how to release it to overcome hurdles in your life.

Even if you are not dealing with an obstacle, to experience unlimited increase and supernatural abundance in your life, you must learn how to identify what you already have and how to use it.

If you are unhappy with where your life is right now, this book was written for you. The book was also written for those who think that something prevents them from becoming all they were created to be. They just know that something is not right because they are not excelling and experiencing success.

Birthday Shoebox

This morning, as I was writing, I was struck by something that happened nine years ago. I say this because my 45th birthday was celebrated last Thursday. In 2010, I had a birthday during one of the most challenging times in our lives. You can read about that in *"From Cameroon to American Citizen: A Journey of Faith."* I had lost my job due to an economic downturn, and being an international worker on a temporary work permit, could not get a different position.

To make matters worse, I had to go back to school to maintain my legal status in the country. That meant I was racking up a great deal of debt on my credit card to pay for tuition without knowing when I would be able to pay it off. In fact, for nine months, I did not earn a dime.

In the midst of all this, on the morning of my birthday, our children - who were eight, five, and three - walked into my room with a shoebox and handed it to me. They had put together a birthday gift for me, and it was no ordinary birthday gift. They had scribed the following note on a piece of paper:

"Dear Daddy, thank you for tickling us and reading our Bible stories. And I wish you a happy birthday,

Love,
Afaamboma,
Ntsongmboma
Elotboma
Xoxoxoxoxoxoxoxoxo"

They had drawn some hearts and decorated the card to the best of their ability. You can see the picture of the card below. They also placed a piece of ceramic art in the box with the words "love, joy, peace" written on it, followed by Galatians 5:22.

When the box was handed to me, and I opened it and read their note, I started crying; even now, as I write, I am crying tears of appreciation because of the strong emotions this evokes. I kept the shoebox because I knew a day would come when I would be standing in front of thousands of people and using this to encourage them to make use of what they already have. The box was fetched from my closet when the thought of what our children did hit me: *You are a beneficiary of little children's thoughtfulness.*

All of us can learn from this type of gesture. The fact that we were going through financial difficulties did not prevent my children from appreciating me and celebrating my birthday. They could have been justified for not doing anything because they "did not have anything." But is that true? They had nothing? The action clearly shows they had *something* because they made use of what they already had.

The highest poverty is not lacking; it is not recognizing what you already have. When you do not make use of what you already have, more will not be given to you. What we have gets multiplied when we use it to render services to other people.

The size of the gift is not as important as the spirit behind the gift. Most people will appreciate a sincere effort more than a fake gift with the wrong spirit behind it, no matter how grand and expensive it is.

I Do Not Have

How often have you heard people say, "I do not have"? Or how often do you state, "I do not have"? This is not only referring to a lack of money, social status, or other resources. Some people feel and say they do not have what it takes to be anything in life. Nothing saps the energy out of us more than thinking or saying that you *do not have*.

Another reason this book was written is to dismantle this notion of lacking that many people express. Many think only in terms of money and material things, but our resources are more than the material – we have both physical and spiritual resources. Unfortunately, since spiritual resources like empathy, love, honesty, etc. cannot be seen and touched, many discount them.

For example, time is one of the most essential resources we have. In fact, time is more important than anything else because we convert time into material things. The truth is that we all have twenty-four hours each day;

therefore, the outcome of our lives is determined by how we use our time.

No wonder one of the greatest complaints people give is lack of time. People lack time to take care of their health, fitness, and wellness. Some have no time to take care of their relationships. Others do not have time for spiritual things. They consider meditation, prayer, and studying the Word of God a waste of time. The admonition that "The fear of the Lord is the beginning of wisdom" (Prov. 9:10) has eluded them. I have read in many books, blogs, and various articles that most successful people meditate in the morning and read something that feeds their minds positively. I even propose that it would be beneficial to you, both in this life and the life to come, to take care of your spiritual life; this is the part of you that will live forever.

In the minds of most people, using "a lack of time" to justify why they are not doing something is good enough reasoning; I believe the issue is more profound than that. Everyone has time to do the things on which their lives depend. You must admit that your priorities are different; therefore, it is not a lack of time preventing you from doing what you should be doing; if it were significant enough in your mind or heart, you would find time for it. As soon as you realize that your life and physical wellbeing may be jeopardized, you'll create an opening in your schedule for that undertaking.

Everybody has something, as the story of the widow's mite demonstrates; we can use it to bless others' lives. We were all born with a purpose and have been equipped with what we need to fulfill that purpose. Along the line, we will need help from other people, but we must take the first step before expecting any help from others.

Therefore, stop saying you do not have and start making use of what you have already; if you look closely enough, you will realize that you have a great deal going for you right now!

The Spiritual Drives the Natural

We live in a secular age, and some people shun anything spiritual, believing that anything spiritual must not be scientific. If they are confusing the spiritual with the religious, they may have a point. The "spiritual" simply means anything that cannot be physically touched, but it is there. We can see, feel, and enjoy the benefits, but cannot measure it in the lab.

Take, for example, integrity, honesty, courage, fear, love, hope, faith, joy, peace, determination, faithfulness, etc. When we see courage, we will know because it leaves trails, and yet we cannot determine if a baby in the womb will be courageous, loving, kind, compassionate, and caring. The fact that we cannot measure these important human attributes does not mean they do not exist.

Without the spiritual, the physical would not be possible. Everything we see in the physical world first existed in someone's mind before it was made in the physical. Therefore, without imagination and proper use of the human mind, there is no room for inventions, innovations, and change.

While the physical may appear to drive everything around us, it is the spiritual that is in the driver's seat. I say this to emphasize the importance of making use of one of the most critical resources we already have: our minds! If you have a sound, functioning mind such that you can dream and come up with great ideas, you are already positioned to make a significant impact on the world around you.

Some have said that whatever your mind can conceive and believe, you can achieve. To their credit, it is not a coincidence that all the great inventions and significant breakthroughs in human history started in the mind. One day, someone figured out in their mind that we could fly, then they went out and started experimenting on this great idea. The idea preceded the experimentation.

The ability to see things with the mind's eyes before these things become physical is called faith. While many people think that faith means a blind leap and trust without evidence or substance, their definition of faith is distorted; it is not faith itself. Faith is an integral part of human life, and we use it all the time.

For example, it takes faith to get on an airplane and fly from one point to another, even though we have little understanding of the laws of aerodynamics. Before you take this act of faith for granted, I want you to think about those who have no confidence in flying. These are individuals who suffer from flight phobia, aviophobia, or aerophobia. No matter what the cause of their fear, in extreme cases, they will not step into an airplane no matter what. They do not believe that the plane can take off and land safely at their destination.

The proper definition: "faith is the substance of things hoped for and the evidence of things not seen." (Heb. 11:1 King James Bible) Or: "faith is confidence in what we hope for and assurance about what we do not see." (Heb. 11:1 NIV)

Based on these definitions, those who do not have faith in flying do not see themselves arriving at their destination; their faithlessness manifested in their refusal to board the plane. On the other hand, those who have faith in flying are certain that they will get to their destination, which is made evident by boarding that airplane.

There are many different types of faith, degrees of faith, as well as objects of faith. This implies that your faith is only as good as the object of your faith because there is no such thing as faith in faith itself.

I bring up this issue of faith because it is at the heart of making use of what you already have and experiencing supernatural growth and increase. You must develop the latitude for the miraculous because, without anticipation and expectation of the extraordinary in your life, you will be limiting yourself.

We will be looking at stories of individuals who experienced miraculous changes in their lives when they used what they already had. I hope that you will read those stories and the associated analysis within the context of a proper understanding of what faith is.

While it is essential to have faith in your giftedness and resources you already possess, the ultimate faith should be in God, your creator. When you trust God to do what He has promised, you will experience the miraculous and the supernatural. Therefore, do not let the physical be the primary driver in your life, instead allow the spiritual to be in charge. When you do this, you will be unstoppable.

A Personal Note

The purpose of this book is to help you focus on what you already have right now to resolve whatever challenge you may be facing. Initially, things will be chaotic, confusing, and unsettling because change is not usually comfortable. But if you hang in there, you will have clarity and a sense of direction.

I mentioned that I moved out of the oil and gas industry. My first reaction was to look for another job as a geologist, but I felt that it was time for me to pursue other things I enjoyed: writing and speaking. However, it took a few detours for me to arrive at this conclusion. I procured my life insurance license and started helping people with their finances, which motivated me to get into the finance industry. Educating people about financial freedom excited me, and still does. But during this process, I realized that I could write and speak.

The next step was to figure out what I already had that could help me move in this direction. Then I realized that I won my first poetry competition in secondary school, yet writing had been something I had shied away from for a while. I already had a doctorate and could teach while writing. Everything started falling into place for me. It has been a slow process, but I have made a lot of progress and am extremely happy that I left the oil and gas industry.

You are reading this book because I decided to make use of what I already had. Most of my teaching is online, demanding a lot of writing, as it is one of the main avenues through which faculty communicates with students. For me, this means that my writing skills are sharpened with each passing day. I also shoot videos for my class, allowing me to practice my speaking, in addition to the face-to-face classes I am currently teaching.

When I look ahead, I am more than excited because, finally, I am in a place where all I have been through is being used to move me to the next place God wants me to be.

My message: Do not be afraid to make use of the resources you already have. You may feel that you have nothing because you think you have to be someone else, but where you are *right now* is the right place, and everything that you have been through has been preparing you for this moment. Your past is not a liability; it is an asset you need to move to the next level.

I want you to read with this mindset, having your eyes open to your existing potential and resources that will move you forward. This will be a journey of personal discovery for you; my prayer is that you will do the deep soul-searching required to unlock your great potential.

Come with me; let us walk together as we allow both past and present heroes to show us how to recognize and use what we already have. Are you ready to dive in? Let's do it!

CHAPTER TWO

Stop Complaining

One of the main objectives of this book is to help you understand why you MUST stop complaining. You may be protesting that this is not fair because complaining soothes your soul. The sad news is that complaining only makes the situation worse because it blinds you to the solutions. It is worth repeating that a solution accompanies every problem or challenge.

It sure feels good to complain because it makes other people feel sympathy for us. Most of us feel good when other people see our point and tell us how much they understand our predicament. However, we remain where we are because, most of the time, when people say they feel for us and wish us well, this is not *the solution* we need. If we want solutions, we should change the way we are currently looking at ourselves and our circumstances.

A recurring theme throughout the rest of this book will be to identify what you already have and use it to solve whatever challenge you may be facing. We will look at different people in the Bible; they had a divine encounter and experienced supernatural provision and increases in their lives because they stopped complaining and started using what they already had to resolve their challenges.

You, too, have a lot of things you are dealing with; here, you'll be presented with the secret to having unlimited provisions and resources to deal with life's challenges.

There are too many excuses people give for not taking care of their spiritual life, finances, education, relationships, career, dreams, vision, ambitions, desires, needs, health, fitness, wellness, etc. The list of things people are supposed to be doing is exhaustive and cannot be enumerated here; you can add your own needs to the list. Some complain of being too young, too old, uneducated, poor, Black, White, unpopular, a felon, minority, reject, abused, weak, disabled, widowed, orphaned, hungry, divorced, unemployed, overqualified, underqualified, and the list goes on. Others complain that their marriage is crumbling because of their mother-in-law (or in-laws in general).

While some feel better for complaining and blaming others, this is all you get: "good feelings." But that doesn't solve problems. Instead, empty complaints worsen the problem because one is admitting a loss of control. Stop complaining and take responsibility.

I heard something the other day that I'll never forget, and I'll paraphrase: "We get angry, not because someone said a mean word to us or mistreated us. We get mad because we already have anger issues, and with mounting pressure, the anger comes out. If we are full of love, when we are pressured, love will come out and nothing else."

Unfortunately, many people blame others and their circumstances or environment, but seldom point the finger at themselves. Those who move forward in victory accept responsibility for their actions, facing them squarely.

Meet Moses

If you think you have complaints that justify not doing what you have been called to do, Moses will eat your lunch. He had more "legitimate" complaints than you can ever come up with, no matter your situation. We will start with Moses because he was being called to do the impossible; his obstacles were legitimate and had the potential to prevent him from doing what he was called to do.

Imagine being called to tell the most influential kingdom on Earth to liberate all the slaves that were making money for the entire economy. You have no army. To make matters worse, you are a fugitive that the king of this country is waiting to hang – and you show up.

That was where Moses was, as God called him to Egypt to ask Pharaoh to set the children of Israel free. The Israelites had been enslaved in Egypt for over 400 years; Moses didn't expect to show up and free them in an instant. That was a preposterous idea; anyone thinking like that must be a lunatic! There was no way Pharaoh would free the very slave labor that was the backbone of his economy.

If you think the task ahead of Moses was an easy one, consider America's Civil War that took more American lives than any other. People would rather die than allow their lifestyle to change, which prompted the Southern states to break away from the union.

You may be thinking that the story of Moses (happening thousands of years ago) has nothing to do with your financial or marital difficulties. Whatever you are facing, I want you to know that the life of Moses can teach you a lot about identifying the solution to a problem, applying it to your life, and experiencing your deliverance.

Moses, who was raised in the palace as the son of Pharaoh's daughter, one day decided to identify with the slaves; he did this by killing an Egyptian slave driver who was mistreating an Egyptian. When Moses learned that his act had been discovered and his life was in danger, he fled Egypt to the land of Midian.

Forty Wasted Years?

Moses would spend the next forty years taking care of his father-in-law's sheep. Wait a minute! What has taking care of sheep got to do with freeing the people of God from the tyranny of Pharaoh? Wouldn't it be smarter if God had used those forty years to help Moses raise and train an army that could be deployed to defeat Pharaoh and free the people? What was God thinking, sending a single individual to confront an entire nation? These questions – and many others – might seem justified, until you look closely at what God had in mind.

Moses did not have to conquer the Egyptian army, which explains why he did not need an army. Second, his assignment was to lead the people out, not free them and keep them in place. Third, Moses would lead the people through the desert, and these forty years navigating through the desert were not wasted.

Lastly, people are, at times, referred to as the "sheep" of God in scripture. Therefore, taking care of sheep was preparing Moses to lead people. As we will see, Moses led millions of Israelites from Egypt to the Promised Land.

Based on God's plan, Moses had the richest resume. First, God needed someone who was a slave and a prince of Egypt to lead his people to freedom. This person must demonstrate that he would not yield to the temptation of the comforts, prestige, and fame that being an Egyptian prince brought. Moses was born by parents who were slaves and adopted by Pharaoh's daughter. Rescued from the crocodile-infested Nile river as an infant, Moses was sent to be raised by his mother. Pharaoh's daughter did not know that she was paying Moses' biological mother to raise him.

We can safely assume that while Moses' mother was raising him, she likely mentioned that he was not an Egyptian, but a Hebrew. This may explain why Moses later chose to suffer alongside the people of God rather than enjoy the temporal pleasures of living in Pharaoh's palace.

Yet, at this point in Moses' life, he was no longer thinking about Egypt because he had been taking care of sheep for forty years, and according to him, he would be a shepherd for life.

Who would blame Moses for thinking like that? After all, he had made the first move to free the people, but God did not support him. When Moses killed the Egyptian and buried him in the sand, it was an indication that he was willing to risk all for God, by placing his own life on the line. God did not respond as Moses had hoped. Instead, Moses became a wanted man, and he fled. Now, he was married and living a peaceful life in exile, and God wanted him to go back to Egypt? No way! God had his chance and did not make use of it; now that Moses was eighty years old, it seemed God was a little too late and should allow the old man to have his much-needed rest.

Where Are You?

Before we proceed, take a critical and close look at your own history. Where have you been, and where are you now? What is it that you are being called to do? Are you afraid to take the next step because you feel unqualified? You are not the first person to think like this; do not be discouraged. Moses, even though he had what it would take to accomplish the task ahead of him, did not feel he was qualified enough to do it.

What you have been through has been preparing you for this moment – stand up and step out. You are qualified to write that book. You are qualified to start that business. You have what it takes to succeed in your marriage.

Instead of thinking that your past is a liability, see it as an asset. Where you are right now is where you are supposed to be. Therefore, stop doubting yourself and believe that you are in the right place at the right time.

Superficially, it appeared as if Moses was in the wrong place, and his experience was not sufficient, yet God chose him because the plan and the timing belong to Him. Trust God with the outcome and stop wishing you had a different set of circumstances. Moses might have felt a little more confident, had he still been in the palace of Pharaoh as a prince with political power. Yet, there he was – a fugitive and shepherd who had spent forty years of his life taking care of sheep.

God Does Not Call "The Qualified"

You may feel that you have wasted your life because what you have been doing seems to have no bearing on the new direction you are being called. What you are not seeing is the divine dimension. The fundamental truth worth repeating is that God does not call "the qualified," *He calls and qualifies.*

This truth can be challenging to understand and apply if care is not taken. Many people have mistaken this to mean that you do nothing, and God just shows up and takes care of everything else. Let's assume that you desire to be a university professor, but you refuse to go to school and get the credentials needed for the job because you think God will call you and qualify you. Or, you are an inventor and make a lousy product and try to sell it to other people, believing that things will just work out because God does not call "the qualified," but He calls the "unqualified" and then qualifies. That is a complete misunderstanding of this truth and will lead to fatalistic thinking, where people feel completely overwhelmed and at the mercy of their circumstances. All they say is, "God's will be done."

When you ask them what God's will is, they have a hard time telling you. Anything that opposes the Word of God has to be opposed by us as well; we do not need more approval if God's Word is crystal clear about what should be happening. There are specific promises in the Word of God for His children, and each time the enemy opposes these promises and prevents them from being fulfilled in our lives, we have to stand against the enemy.

When we say that God does not call "the qualified" but calls the "unqualified" and qualifies them, it means that God's way of evaluating where we have been, who we are, and what we have or do not have differs from that of the world. Therefore, we need to trust God to accomplish whatever He initiates in our lives. This is where it becomes imperative to know that God is leading you and *not just your ego, greed, or presumptuousness.*

If God is indeed calling you to do a certain thing, you are qualified to do it and will succeed, because He can do whatever He sets out to accomplish. The issue of qualification hinges on our interpretation of what we mean by that. Take the case of Moses. If an arms invasion was what would have freed the people, then Moses was not qualified. But that was not God's plan.

If you feel discouraged, frustrated, or as if you have been blocked, it may be because you have a different idea of the plan. It is time to reassess your situation and become the actor in the good, the bad, and the ugly that you have been through; all of this was in preparation for the next phase of your journey.

When Nothing Makes Sense

We are talking about complaining here, especially when nothing makes sense to you. Of course, little makes sense when you are sent on a mission without what you believe you need to succeed. Moses must have felt like this; it must have made little sense for him to be asked to free millions of people from the strongest nation on Earth.

Moses was not just going to go because he had been asked. He would go to the complaint book and pull out every imaginable distraction. Here is how the conversation between Moses and God went:

> "And the Lord said: 'I have surely seen the oppression of My people who are in Egypt and have heard their cry because of their taskmasters, for I know their sorrows. So I have come down to deliver them out of the hand of the Egyptians, and to bring them up from that land to a good and large land, to a land flowing with milk and honey, to the place of the Canaanites and the Hittites and the Amorites and the Perizzites and the Hivites and the Jebusites. Now therefore, behold, the cry of the children of Israel has come to Me, and I have also seen the oppression with which the Egyptians oppress them. Come now, therefore, and I will send you to Pharaoh that you may bring My people, the children of Israel, out of Egypt.'" (Exod. 3:7-10 New King James Version)

The first time Moses tried to free the Israelites from slavery, he was the one who initiated it. Part of the reason he failed may be that the timing was not right.

Whatever the reason, Moses was not interested in failing again.

But this time, there was a huge difference. God was initiating the process and was the one sending Moses on a deliverance mission. Moses thought he was not ready for this task. Forty years of taking care of sheep had convinced Moses he was nothing more than a shepherd. Moses' response speaks volumes:

> "But Moses said to God, 'Who am I that I should go to Pharaoh, and that I should bring the children of Israel out of Egypt?'" (Exod. 3:11 NKJV)

We must spend some time on this fundamental question that Moses asked. Who am I? That was a legitimate question that needed to be answered because the way forward for Moses depended on the answer. Unfortunately, Moses had forgotten his story. His mother must have told him that when he was born, a decree from Pharaoh mandated every male child born into a Hebrew family be killed. But when Moses was born, his parents refused to hand him over to be killed because they saw something in him. Maybe they thought he would be the Deliverer. His parents did not wait for the laws to change, but instead, made use of what they had. They could at least hide the baby for three months. It is interesting that, while other parents were having their male children murdered, the parents of Moses risked their lives to hide him. They did not know how things would play out, but they took the first step.

After hiding Moses for three months, they could no longer hide him. Again, his parents saw beyond their obstacles and came up with a plan of action, not knowing the outcome. We see his parents still making use of what they already had. While the other parents were crying out against the law that was killing their children, the Moses' parents were busy making a basket. After the basket was completed, they sealed it with tar to make it waterproof.

Then his parents did the unthinkable. They placed the baby in the basket, handed it to his older sister, Miriam, so that she could place the basket in the crocodile-infested Nile river. What were his parents thinking when they put their child in harm's way like that? Was it not a form of abuse and neglect? Which parents, in their right minds, would place a three-month-old baby in a basket and toss it in the river? Their actions did not make any sense at all.

The baby could have quickly been eaten by crocodiles or died from dehydration or heat stroke from the sun. But Moses' parents understood that to keep something, you must be willing to give it up. They gave up their son and ended up keeping him. They not only kept him, but they were being paid to raise their son. Can you imagine how that must have felt? Not only was the life of their son spared, but he was also given back to them *with pay*.

When Moses was placed in the Nile river by his sister, Pharaoh's daughter happened to be in the river bathing and heard the cries of the baby. She instructed that the baby be brought to her. She not only rescued him but, even after learning he was a Hebrew baby, adopted Moses as her son.

She was thinking aloud about who would raise the baby for her when Miriam stepped in and suggested that she knew a woman who could help. She brought her mother without revealing her identity. That is how the Moses' parents saved the life of their son and preserved him to one day become the Deliverer.

But where Moses was right now (after eighty years had gone by), he seemed to have forgotten all this. Moses no longer remembered his parents telling him he was not an Egyptian, but a Hebrew, and that there was a promise from God to deliver them from the bondage of slavery.

God's Patience

When God starts something, He completes it. Moses thought that doubting himself and complaining that he was the wrong person for the job would discourage God from sending him on this crucial mission. God would not let Moses talk himself out of this critical assignment:

> "So He said, 'I will certainly be with you. And this shall be a sign to you that I have sent you: When you have brought the people out of Egypt, you shall serve God on this mountain.'

> Then Moses said to God, 'Indeed, when I
> come to the children of Israel and say to them,
> "The God of your fathers has sent me to you,"
> and they say to me, "What is His name?" what
> shall I say to them?'
>
> And God said to Moses, 'I AM WHO I AM.'
> And He said, 'Thus you shall say to the children
> of Israel, "I AM has sent me to you."'" (Exod.
> 3:12-14 NKJV)

It is incredible how patient God was with Moses, who
kept moving from one complaint to another, even
after God has promised and assured him He would
be with him. Does this sound familiar? Has Jesus not
given us the same promise that He will always be with
us, even to the end of the age? Has God not made
our bodies His temple and now dwells in us? Has He
not promised that He would never leave nor forsake
us? Besides all these promises, nothing can separate
us from the love of God. "Nothing" means the devil,
demons, principalities, powers, spiritual wickedness
in high places, poverty, joblessness, homelessness,
abandonment, etc. Are we aware of this? How does
our speech reflect our understanding and acceptance
of these precious, unfailing promises of God?

Thank God for His patience because He did not
chastise Moses but kept answering his questions and
dismantling his complaints and doubts. By the end of
Exodus 3:1-22, Moses is still not convinced that going
to Egypt is a good idea; he was looking for any possible
way to get out of the assignment.

Where are you? What is holding you back? Have you been conditioned by your upbringing, teachers, and life experience to think that you do not have what it takes to be all you were created to be? There is much about you that you did not choose, and these are the very things you think are a liability and are preventing you from excelling. Those things you did not select for yourself are assets. Now is the time for you to embrace your skin color, ethnicity, when and where you were born. You have one life and were born at the right time and in the right place. Those who make a difference in their generation are those who recognize that they belong. Without a sense of mission and purpose, you will just drift through life without achieving anything.

What Do You Have?

The promises and assurances God gave to Moses were not enough (according to him), and he kept coming up with one reason after another to try to get out of the assignment. The next thing that Moses said makes a lot of sense, but it is not good enough:

> "Then Moses answered and said, 'But suppose they will not believe me or listen to my voice; suppose they say, "The Lord has not appeared to you."' So, the Lord said to him, 'What is that in your hand?' He said, 'A rod.' And He said, 'Cast it on the ground.' So, he cast it on the ground, and it became a serpent; Moses fled from it. Then the Lord said to Moses, 'Reach out your hand and take it by the tail' (and he reached out his hand and caught it, and

> it became a rod in his hand), 'that they may
> believe that the Lord God of their fathers, the
> God of Abraham, the God of Isaac, and the
> God of Jacob, has appeared to you.'" (Exod.
> 4:1-5 NKJV)

It appears Moses was not getting it at all. He was not willing to go to Egypt because he was afraid for his life. Now God had to convince Moses that he was the man for the job. Moses already had the solution in his hand, but he was not aware of it. The rod in Moses' hand had been with him for a while, but he had taken it for granted. Who wouldn't? Of what use was a shepherd's rod if not to take care of sheep? Moses was letting conventional wisdom and his experience blind him to the great potential in his rod.

Before now, Moses thought political power was what he needed to free the Hebrews, but that failed. This failure forced Moses to become a shepherd in a foreign country for forty years. During those years, Moses had convinced himself that he was not the man for the job because his activities appeared to have nothing to do with freeing his people. Had it been that Moses was in some military academy learning military strategies and how to invade a country and free people, this would have made sense to him. But God wanted to let Moses know that the forty years of shepherding were not wasted. That is why he asked Moses about what he had in his hand.

It is important to note that God asked Moses to name what he was holding *before* He transformed it into a snake. God wanted him to know that forty years shepherding had not been wasted, but instead, had something to do with the assignment. When we give over to God that which we consider ordinary and mundane, God can make it into whatever He deems fit.

To Moses, the shepherd rod was just a dead piece of wood that symbolized his new status as a shepherd. This rod constantly reminded him of where his life had been spent over the past forty years; it was a concrete summation of his life at that moment. God brought Moses up to speed, reminding him that the past was not wasted and that he would use it to secure a different future.

This profound message has the potential to transform you. I am saying this because many people always want to fix themselves before coming to God. You do not need to do this because you cannot fix yourself. It is a fact that Moses had spent forty years taking care of sheep, and all he had was a rod. He needed nothing else for God to do what He wanted to do through him.

You, too, do not need fancy equipment, different skin pigmentation, country of birth, parents, career, or whatever you think you need as a prerequisite for God to use you. The message to Moses was clear: the past forty years have not been wasted and are now going to be used to bring forth a mighty miracle.

There Is No Good Complaint

God powerfully demonstrated to Moses that he was the right man for the job, but Moses was not getting it. Nothing God did seemed to work, even after turning the rod into a snake, and then turning it back into a rod. What is it that Moses wanted God to do? Let's look at their conversation:

> "Then Moses said to the Lord, 'O my Lord, I am not eloquent, neither before nor since You have spoken to Your servant; but I am slow of speech and slow of tongue.'
>
> So, the Lord said to him, 'Who has made man's mouth? Or who makes the mute, the deaf, the seeing, or the blind? Have not I, the Lord? Now, therefore, go, and I will be with your mouth and teach you what you shall say.'
>
> But he said, 'O my Lord, please send by the hand of whomever else You may send.'
>
> So, the anger of the Lord was kindled against Moses, and He said: 'Is not Aaron the Levite your brother? I know that he can speak well. And look, he is also coming out to meet you. When he sees you, he will be glad in his heart. Now you shall speak to him and put the words in his mouth. And I will be with your mouth and with his mouth, and I will teach you what you shall do. So, he shall be your spokesman to the people. And he himself shall be as a mouth for you, and you shall be to him as God. And

> you shall take this rod in your hand, with which
> you shall do the signs."" (Exod. 4:10-17 NKJV)

It seems that Moses had some legitimate complaints. For example, who would fault him for being slow of speech? If you are slow of speech, you are slow of speech. Moses was not faking it. The only issue is that he used his slowness of speech as an excuse to back out of the assignment God was giving him. Instead of looking for solutions, his complaints from the get-go were to get him out of God's assignment. Moses was doing all within his power not to go to Egypt. But God would not have any of it.

God was bent on sending him because Moses was born for this task, and he was not going to complain his way out of it. The handwriting was on the wall. God had his man and would not let him slip away like that.

God does not want us to carry out assignments for which He has not already made provision. That is why he pointed out to Moses that his brother Aaron would be his spokesperson. The assignment on which God was sending Moses was not as a master orator. Moses did not need the skills of an orator to deliver the message to Pharaoh.

How often do you self-sabotage in a project or task by coming up with some ridiculous requirements? Most of the things we think we need to be happy, contented and fulfilled are bogus. We have allowed the marketing agencies, friends, and other people to determine what we need. This explains why we can never catch up because, just as soon as we succumb to the newest fashion trend, a newer one pops up. This never-ending rat race of playing catch-up does not work. It is time to get out of this mindset and learn how just to be you.

Complaining is so detrimental – you should do all within your power to stop this habit. Let the encounter between Moses and God be an inspiration for you to stop complaining because you can't simultaneously complain and look for a solution. While Moses was busy complaining, he forgot the rod he had, even forgetting that his brother could be of great help.

I have yet to meet anybody who complained their way out of a problem to a solution. All complaining does is make an already bad situation worse. One complaint only leads to another, because the purpose of complaining is to avoid looking for a solution, rather than doing something to correct the situation.

Not doing anything is a dead end, and dead ends should be avoided at all costs. What has complaining done for you lately? When you complain, and people feel sorry for you, and you feel sorry for yourself, how does this help improve your situation? There are always solutions tied into whatever situation, problem, or challenge you may be facing. But you must push yourself to go past the problem or obstacle and tap into the solution.

Who Are You?

In the passage we just examined, Moses asked the following question: "Who am I that I should go to Pharaoh, and that I should bring the children of Israel out of Egypt?" (Exod. 3:11 NKJV) It seems Moses had forgotten who he was because if he *knew who he was*, he would not have asked this question. When you forget who you are – God's child – it is impossible to make use of what you already have; you will not recognize it. There is nothing more destructive than self-doubt!

The other day, I heard a story that illustrates this very clearly. An ornithologist went to visit the farm of one of his friends and saw something that caught his attention. An eagle was scratching around with the other chickens, just like a chicken. This sight troubled the ornithologist, who asked his friend the history of the eagle. The friend told him he had found the eagle egg and had placed it in a nest to be incubated by one of the hens. Then the eagle hatched with other chicken eggs. After the eggs hatched, the hen raised the eagle with her own chicks; the eagle thought he was a chicken and behaved like one. According to the farmer, the eagle had never attempted to fly and would never fly because all he knew was how to be a chicken.

The ornithologist told the farmer, "Once an eagle, always an eagle." He let his friend know that it was just a matter of time, and the eagle would take to the air and fly away. To demonstrate his point, the ornithologist picked up the eagle and threw it upwards, but it did not fly. The farmer triumphantly repeated his belief that the eagle would never fly because it was hatched with other chickens, ate with other chickens, and lived beside nothing but other chickens. Therefore, the eagle was an eagle externally, but a chicken internally.

The ornithologist cautioned his friend not to be too confident in his position because he would return the next day and prove that the eagle was born to soar. He maintained that feeding an eagle chicken feed and raising it as a chicken does not make an eagle into a chicken.

The next day the ornithologist showed up before sunrise. He picked up the eagle and pointed its face towards the sun. Immediately the sun rose, he let go of the eagle, and it flew away and never returned. The eagle had been awakened from slumber and discovered that he was not made to scramble for crumbs of food on the ground with chickens. He was not ground-bound; he was created for the skies.

Just because someone has told you that you cannot do something does not mean you cannot do it. The fact that you were born and raised under certain circumstances does not mean you are at the mercy of those circumstances. All your life, you might have been hanging around with certain people that have conditioned you to think that you are just like them. You are not what other people think or even say that you are, because the opinion they have of you is only an opinion. What truly matters is your opinion about yourself.

You Must Name What You Have

There is power in a name because a name defines what something is. That is part of the reason why we have so much fighting over gender identity. If what we called ourselves did not matter, there wouldn't be huge controversy over whether someone should be called a girl/woman or boy/man. It is interesting how some are even trying to take a position of neutrality, in the so-called "binary gender" category. Those seeking to change their gender, and insisting that they are called something else, recognize the power of proper naming, but forget that just because you call yourself something, it does not necessarily make you that thing.

Naming what you have provides proper identification of what you already have; if you cannot call it by name, you cannot use it. When you identify what you have, it is then – and only then – that you will use it properly.

When Conventional Wisdom Does Not Make Sense

Most of us operate by conventional wisdom, and rightfully so because this is what we have been taught and have learned from others and our environment. For example, when you get up in the morning, you brush your teeth, take a bath, eat breakfast, and go about your day. Then at the end of the day, you go to sleep. Everybody does this, and it is expected to be like that. There may be some exceptions, but most people get out of bed, eat, sleep, and do it repeatedly.

There are many areas of our lives that are in automatic mode, and things will probably roll like that, but a time comes when conventional wisdom does not make any sense at all. *If you want to experience increase and supernatural growth, you must let go of conventional wisdom.*

For example, conventional wisdom taught Moses that the rod of a shepherd was only used to take care of sheep and to carry. There was zero possibility of that rod becoming a snake, but all this changed when Moses had an encounter with God.

That which Moses was trying to neglect and discard became the very thing that God used to accomplish a mighty deliverance. Was Moses right in saying he was not qualified? I think he was because it was a manifestation of humility, but finally, Moses moved from saying he was not qualified to accepting the call to do the job.

Many of us stay too long in the "not qualified" parking lot. It is time to take off and do what you have been called to do. How long are you going to allow conventional wisdom to prevent you from moving forward?

If, for instance, your husband cheated on you and divorced you over ten years ago, instead of moving forward with your life, you are still angry and bitter. Each time his name is mentioned, your blood pressure goes up. Conventional wisdom dictates that you take revenge. That's what you are hoping and praying for: that your former husband should suffer some misfortune. In short, you want something terrible to happen to him because he caused you so much pain.

Don't you know that refusing to forgive is like drinking poison and hoping the other person dies?

Remember: God will not forgive your sins if you do not forgive others. He makes clear that vengeance is His, and He will repay those who have done evil to you. Could you be so troubled and miserable because you are trying to *be God*, attempting to do that which only He can do?

Conventional wisdom dictates that if you are born within a particular socio-economic group, you will not escape poverty and will remain at the bottom of society. You must allow the lack in your life to fuel you to do more and escape poverty. Many people use the very thing that was meant to keep them down to rise to the top.

Les Brown

I immediately think about Les Brown, who was born in an abandoned building; his mother gave him up for adoption when he was born; he was never able to meet his biological mother or father. In elementary school, he was labeled as educable mentally retarded (EMR). The future for a person like him was bleak. To make matters worse, Les Brown is African American and grew up during segregation. There was no indication he would ever be anything. But in high school, one of his teachers left an impression on him that changed his life forever.

He walked into the classroom, and the teacher asked him to solve a problem; he responded that he could not. The teacher asked why, and he answered that he was educable mentally retarded. This teacher was not going to let conventional wisdom dictate his interaction with this student. He told him to come to the board and solve the problem anyway. Then he said these words that forever changed Les Brown's life: "Don't you ever say that again. Someone's opinion of you does not have to become your reality." Les Brown went on from there to become a successful politician and is one of the most sought-after motivational speakers. He has used his story to inspire and motivate millions of people to take ownership of what they already have and maximize it.

Nick Vujicic

Another person who comes to mind is Nick Vujicic, who has been to over forty-two countries – even though he was born without legs and arms. The very thing that was meant to keep him down has brought him before audiences all over the world. Instead of allowing conventional wisdom to dictate his response, Nick chose to allow God to make use of what he already had, and that is not being like any "normal person."

Conventional wisdom is centered on what is normal and fitting within whatever boxes society has defined for us. But to experience supernatural increase and breakthroughs, fulfilling the purpose of your life, it is imperative that you get out of the box. Moses and all the other people who left an impression on human history got out of the box. Some of these people threw away the box, and this allowed them to tap into endless possibilities.

Stephen Covey

Stephen Covey is the author of the popular book "The 7 Habits of Highly Effective People", selling more than 25 million copies. He told a story in his book that is worth repeating here.

One day he was going to the airport, and suddenly they ran into a traffic jam because of road construction. It occurred to him that he was going to be late for his flight if nothing was done. Conventional wisdom dictated that he sit in the taxi, get agitated, and let his blood pressure rise. He might even curse and hiss at the construction company for messing up his plans for the day. There are a thousand and one different things he could have said, but nothing was going to help him get out of the situation.

Mr. Covey told the taxi driver he was going to get out of the taxi and redirect the traffic so they could help everybody, and in the process, help him get to the airport on time. The taxi driver thought he was just joking and was flabbergasted when he got out of the car and started directing the traffic. His effort paid off, and they got to the airport on time. He did not miss his flight because he made use of what he already had, instead of sitting there and complaining and feeling helpless.

Next time you are in a tight spot and the temptation to grumble and complain hits you, take a deep breath and focus on solutions because there are always solutions. The problem with most people is that they do not want to go through the process, because seeking a solution will require some hard work and risk-taking.

We are living in a generation that prefers comfort and pleasure above all else. The mantra is, "If it feels good, do it, do not deny yourself anything as long as it brings you pleasure." Any talk about delayed gratification, sacrifice, and going through pain is discarded. Is it any surprise that we are one of the most affluent generations, yet the most miserable? The family size is reducing; however, the size of houses and cars is increasing. The happiness, satisfaction, and contentment index of many people is declining, even though they earn more money and have access to faster and better technological advances.

America's Founding Fathers

The United States of America is a country that would never have existed if the Founding Fathers allowed conventional wisdom to lead them. Just like Moses going before Pharaoh – who was the most powerful king on Earth – and asking for the Hebrews to be freed, the Founding Fathers were asking the most powerful kingdom to stop taxation without representation. This was a challenge that many thought would go nowhere. The British had the most powerful army and had been fighting for hundreds of years and could easily crush any rebellion. Well, the rest is history, because we have a nation today called the United States of America as proof of what can be achieved when conventional wisdom is ignored.

An endless list of people chose to follow unconventional wisdom and achieved many things that are noble and worthy to emulate. But we will now move forward to a topic that is a thorny one in the US: racism.

Slavery And Racism

These days the issue of racism, driven by a legacy of slavery and mistreatment of Blacks in the US, keeps making news headlines. Let me state categorically: there is no justification for the heinous and despicable things done to African Americans under the guise of slavery. Even after slavery ended, the Jim Crow laws and segregation in the South did not make things any better. The lynchings, murders, torture, and all the other evil perpetrated against African Americans should be condemned and rejected by all. Conventional wisdom demands that African Americans should not only never forget, but should remain in anger, bitterness, resentment, and animosity towards the Caucasians who did this evil to them. While this is an incredibly charged and divisive issue, it is crucial to understand that following conventional wisdom is taking the low road and will never deliver the healing and restoration needed.

Those who have been hurt should take the high road, forgiving, and making use of what they already have. It is possible to allow a history of slavery to become the stepping stone to bigger and better things, but the continuous focus on the pain and hurt is a distraction they cannot afford.

The proposal that I am presenting here, which is well-articulated in the book "*Racism, Where is Your Sting: An Orthodox Solution to the Beginning and the End of Racism,*" is not one that I expect to be popular. The majority is wrong most of the time, and my intention is **not to appeal to the majority**.

I moved to the United States of America, more than 8000 miles from my country of birth, because I wanted to get a good education. That meant I had to leave behind my parents, siblings, and many other things I held dear. Living in the diaspora has its numerous challenges; but, I am leveraging my history and all my experiences to write and inspire other people to become aware of the greater potential in their own lives – and to take action.

There have been many ups and downs, failures, and setbacks on the way. For example, I have been laid off twice, and each time it took a while to get back into the workforce. I chose not to blame others, but to look at the opportunities as a time of reflection and reinvention of myself. This has pushed me onto the path I am on right now, that of writing and speaking! I have found my voice, and I am singing my song. It took me leaving my country of birth and traveling halfway across the world to do that!

Conventional wisdom dictates that a geoscientist like myself should be working in the oil and gas industry or some geology-related profession. I defied that "wisdom" to pursue writing because a part of me says I am not cut out for that. What keeps me going is the fact that I believe in this message of making use of what I already have. In my case, I have a good education and many experiences that I can use to inspire, equip, and motivate other people.

Joseph, The Unlikely Leader

Before I propose a solution to the history of slavery, discrimination, and racism in the US, I would like you to meet Joseph, who was hated by his brothers. The brothers allowed their envy and jealousy to force them to sell Joseph as a slave to Egypt. They wanted him to die so that his dreams of someday becoming a leader would not materialize.

But the brothers did not know that after thirteen years, Joseph would come to their rescue in a significant way. A famine hit the land, and his brothers made their way to Egypt to buy grain, where they met him. Joseph was now the prime minister of Egypt with the power to take away their lives.

Conventional wisdom dictates that Joseph should punish his brothers for the heinous crime they committed against him. It was payback time, and

Joseph had the power to do and undo, yet, he did the unthinkable; he chose to forgive his brothers. His response:

> "Then Joseph said to his brothers, 'I am Joseph; does my father still live?' But his brothers could not answer him, for they were dismayed in his presence. And Joseph said to his brothers, 'Please come near to me.' So they came near. Then he said: 'I am Joseph, your brother, whom you sold into Egypt. But now, do not, therefore, be grieved or angry with yourselves because you sold me here; for God sent me before you to preserve life. For these two years, the famine has been in the land, and there are still five years in which there will be neither plowing nor harvesting. **And God sent me before you to preserve a posterity for you in the earth, and to save your lives by a great deliverance. So now it was not you who sent me here, but God; and He has made me a father to Pharaoh, and lord of all his house, and a ruler throughout all the land of Egypt.'**" (Gen. 45:3-8 NKJV) (Note: emphases in bold are my own.)

This passage of scripture is one of the most moving to me. Can you imagine what was running through Joseph's mind, and the restraint he employed in talking to his brothers? He said, "do not, therefore, be grieved or angry with yourselves because you sold me here; for God sent me before you to preserve life." (Gen. 45:5 NKJV) Does this make sense? Why was

Joseph not demanding justice? He even said something stranger by encouraging his brothers not to feel sorry for themselves for doing what they did. Was Joseph suffering from denial and self-delusion? How could he not only let the guilty go free but want them not to blame themselves?

Joseph made use of the very thing that was meant to destroy him. The slavery that his brothers had sold him into became the very thing that God was using to save the whole family.

In short, Joseph made another declaration that is mind-boggling when he said, "So now it was not you who sent me here, but God." (Gen 45:8 NKJV) This is going too far! Where was God when his brothers caught him, bound him, and threw him in the well? Where was God when his brothers pulled him out of the well and sold him for twenty pieces of silver? How could God allow Joseph to be thrown in prison for refusing to commit adultery? He was a slave with no rights and would have been justified if he obeyed the instructions of his owner's wife by having sex with her. But Joseph refused, and this landed him in prison.

Do you think Joseph was not homesick and fearing for his life through this ordeal? Do you think it was not painful for him to suffer for thirteen years? Why did God allow it to happen? We can ask why all day, but the good news is that Joseph decided to go past the "why" and trusted God to make something beautiful out of the colossal mess.

I say this to declare that conventional wisdom does not work because it perpetuates the problem. Conventional wisdom may contain some sense, but it is limited because it keeps people bound. The African Americans whose ancestors were betrayed by their own brothers on the African continent and sold into slavery, then forcefully brought to the Caribbean and the Americas, have every reason to be angry. They should not be faulted for asking for justice, reparations, and even vengeance.

All these reactions are driven by conventional wisdom; allowing that *alone* to guide us, may get us stuck. While it may make sense to us, it is not the complete picture. This explains why we are still dealing with the issue of racism, hate, and vengeance.

Politicians who want quick votes keep stoking these fires and reopening the wounds repeatedly in the name of justice and fairness. These politicians and many other people who keep stoking these fires pretend they care, but they do not. They are more concerned about power, money, and fame for themselves. Lining their pockets is more important to them than a holistic and permanent solution to this scourge in American history.

It is time to allow unconventional wisdom to do its work. This does not mean we will deny the past or pretend it was not painful, but we must choose the higher road, and that is the path of forgiveness. It is imperative to see God's work in all this. Yes, we were sold, mistreated, lynched, abused and brutalized, but GOD sent us here to save many.

The devil always means it for evil when he uses people to commit heinous crimes against other people. This includes what happened in the Americas. While some people tried to use the Bible to cloak this barbaric, despicable, and heinous act, it stuck out like a sore thumb. There is no justification under the sun for what happened. That said, the way forward is to see the hand of God in all this, to begin to make good out of what the enemy meant for evil. It can be as small as acknowledging that you are born a US citizen.

When you watch the news and see the thousands trying to cross into the US through the southern border because they believe the US is a land of opportunity, it should make every US citizen grateful. Each year millions of people worldwide try to move to the US by participating in the Diversity Visa (DV) Lottery. They are willing to do whatever it takes to become part of the US.

You may think that the mistreatment and all the African Americans have gone through pales compared to being US citizens. You are right and wrong at the same time because you are not comparing apples to apples. It is impossible to mix light and darkness or evil and good because they are diametrically opposed to each other. Such comparisons again are driven by conventional wisdom, which feeds off self-pity, hate, fear, regret, revenge, and vengeance.

There is a better way, and now is the time to adopt it. What the enemy meant for evil can be used for the good of the country. Those who want to truly heal must develop a heart of gratitude for being here in the US. In so doing, they will enjoy true freedom. They must reject the dictates of conventional wisdom that insists that they have only a history of slavery, exploitation, lynching, segregation, and racism. Say no to conventional wisdom and yes to unconventional wisdom by embracing the history and using it to fulfill your purpose.

Your ancestors might have been brought here for the wrong reasons, just as Joseph was taken to Egypt, but there was a bigger purpose, and I am beckoning you to step into that more significant purpose. America needs your giftedness, and the world needs you to show how people can heal from the hurt. We are living in a world filled with hurting, sick, and hopeless people, and they cannot wait to hear the message of hope and redemption you are about to bring.

You can boldly declare, like Joseph, that it is God who sent you here, and not your African brothers who sold you to the Europeans who brought you to the Americas. Oh, what joy and freedom will flood your soul when you understand that God can make use of the good, the bad, and the ugly in your life. This will bring about holistic transformation in your life and the lives of all other people associated with you. Then the country will truly begin to heal, and true justice will be done.

Right now, we are fueling evil, and the devil is happy that there is still hate, anger, and the desire for vengeance. How is all this negative energy helping us as a country? It is not, and we must break out of it.

Lastly, you may want to dismiss what I have said here because, as some have already said: I was not born here and do not understand the pain, hurt and inhumane treatment that African Americans have been through and continue to go through. Well, don't let conventional wisdom lead you. Who said you must be born in the US to point the country towards the light?

When light shines in a dark room, everybody in that room recognizes it; if they were doing something wrong, they immediately try to adjust. Did the lights come on for you? Are you feeling uncomfortable because a part of you is saying that what you have read might work? If so, I strongly recommend that you consider walking in the light of unconventional wisdom. Choose forgiveness, and it will bring you much-needed hope, love, healing, and peace. Yes, you can, and you should!

You Are Not Helpless

I am wrapping up this chapter with the bold statement that you are not helpless. Many times, you will think and even feel that you are helpless, but that is just what you think and feel. Do not forget that when these feelings of helplessness and hopelessness are trying to drown you, you have allowed conventional wisdom to take the upper hand.

The danger of complaining is that it places conventional wisdom in full control of your life. This implies that you become a victim of your circumstances; instead of strengthening your resolve to look for a solution, you have empowered the situation to your detriment.

There is nothing more devastating to your ability to overcome obstacles than complaining. While there are temporary relief and comfort, it turns to generalized fear, helplessness, and hopelessness. You must break free from its grip on your life. *Avoid people who constantly complain – there are professional complainers!* If it's not raining, they whine about the drought and dust. When it rains, they grumble of flooding and mud. The weather to them is always wrong, no matter what time of day or year. These individuals have a hard time staying positive. They should be avoided like the plague.

The only way you can stop complaining *is to stop complaining.* You are not helpless because there is always a solution in your hand. Just like Moses, whose shepherd's rod appeared insignificant until the Divine encounter, there is a "shepherd's rod" in your hand – and you should use it. This might be your past experiences, history, or whatever you have been through. Do not neglect it, because where you have been has prepared you for this moment forward.

CHAPTER THREE

Open Your Eyes

What do you do when faced with an obstacle that appears to be insurmountable? I say "appears" because perception is everything. You have received a vision and are faithfully executing it, then suddenly, you hit a roadblock and do not know what to do. Your business took off and had been going well, then things started going south, and you do not know how to get back on track. Before you got married, you were certain that you had met the right mate, but now it seems you are married to a total stranger; your marriage is falling apart, and there appears to be no help in sight.

You have been pushed between a rock and a hard place, and it appears there is no way out. To make matters worse, this dire situation in which you find yourself has nothing to do with you at all because you have been faithful in doing your part to the best of your ability. Your mate decided to cheat on you and break your marriage vows, not because of anything wrong that you have done. They just decided to satisfy their desires without factoring in your marriage, and now you are devastated. You have been a stay-at-home mom and invested most of your adult life in your children, but they have turned their backs on you, with no remorse.

Perception and Attitude are Everything

What I mean by "perception and attitude" refers to how you see life. It is your paradigm or your worldview. We all have a worldview that influences how we view life and respond to circumstances and situations we go through.

Life is not a piece of cake – you will be faced with one challenge or another. Some have said that at any point in your life, if you are not climbing out of a valley towards a mountaintop, you are descending from the mountaintop towards a valley. Wherever you are may matter less than you think, because the valley has its advantages and disadvantages, just as the mountaintop does.

In the valley, you are exposed to flooding, but these floods bring sediments that are deposited on the river flood plains. The sediments produce alluvial soils that are very fertile. Each time there is a flood, these soils are replenished with new alluvium, which keeps them perpetually fertile. This explains why most ancient civilizations started on the flood plains of rivers such as the Nile, Ganges, Tigris, and Euphrates.

On the mountaintop, you have clear visibility and can see far ahead. Metaphorically, it implies that you can see into the future and have an intuition about what is coming. This ability to see into the future comes with its own risk, just like the strong winds that you have on the mountaintop. If you cannot handle what you see, it can be so overwhelming that you give up completely and do nothing.

While many people like to talk of mountaintop experiences, you cannot stay on top of the mountain for long; sooner or later you will run out of supplies. The beauty on top of the mountain is great, but the resources for which you need to live are in the valley below. This implies that you need not stay on the mountaintop for a long time. Those who have climbed the Himalayas will tell you that when you get to the summit, you had better start going down, or you will be buried on the mountain, as many have been.

While the valley may be the dumping ground for all the runoff from the mountain and all the weathering products, the valley has figured out how to use these dumped materials to make it an oasis for agricultural productivity. *The issue is not whether you should be living on the mountaintop or in the valley. You need both the valley and the mountain. What determines the outcome is your perception and attitude.*

When you understand that each phase in your life serves a purpose, you will no longer focus on where you are, but on why you are there. The right attitude will make the mountain – as well as the valley – work for you; both are essential in your life.

Climbing up any mountain is never easy, but if you fail to put in the energy and effort, you cannot enjoy the beautiful view and fresh air at the top. That said, it's also easier to go down towards the valley than to climb up. This explains why streams flow downhill – not uphill. The streams are just making use of what they already have by taking advantage of the force of gravity. When you are on a hill, gravity is pulling you towards the valley. Therefore, streams just go for this free ride.

It's nearly impossible for a stream to flow uphill; it takes a lot of work to happen! Dam construction makes it possible for streams to flow against gravity, but this is unnatural and poses many risks. The pressure that is built in front of the dam by the accumulated water is the kinetic energy of the flowing water transformed into potential energy.

When released unexpectedly, this potential energy causes flooding downstream, in some cases leading to death and destruction of property. You do not want to go against the flow, because you will need more energy and will open yourself up to potential hazards.

Going against the flow is when you refuse to identify and make use of what you already have.

There is nothing more freeing and empowering then being you. There is a great danger in trying to be someone else: you'll end up an imitation, and people do not like imitations.

Therefore, no matter where you are, open your eyes and see the opportunities all around you. That is a winning attitude and helps you thrive, no matter where you find yourself.

Pushed Against the Wall

Life is full of twists and turns, and as we have seen, you will need the right perspective and attitude to keep moving. It does not matter where you are; if you don't open your eyes to look both internally and externally, you will get stuck. That said, being on an excellent course and doing everything right will not prevent obstacles from being placed in your path. Some of these barriers will be natural, and others will be erected by your enemies.

Moses and his people had barely left Egypt when they came across the first of many obstacles they would overcome before reaching the Promised Land. They were between a rock and a hard place, not because of any fault of their own. They had obeyed the instruction to start the march towards the Promised Land, and the route had been chosen by God. Yet, they were now facing the Red Sea, without boat or ferry to get across. To make matters worse, the Egyptian army was in hot pursuit!

Uh-oh! Some people might have thought it was a bad idea in the first place, as trying to leave without destroying the Egyptian army made little sense. Now this army was trying to force them back to Egypt. The people operated on conventional wisdom:

"And when Pharaoh drew near, the children of Israel lifted their eyes, and behold, the Egyptians marched after them. So they were very afraid, and the children of Israel cried out to the Lord. Then they said to Moses, 'Because there were no graves in Egypt, have you taken us away to die in the wilderness? Why have you so dealt with us, to bring us up out of Egypt? Is this not the word that we told you in Egypt, saying, **Let us alone that we may serve the Egyptians? For it would have been better for us to serve the Egyptians than that we should die in the wilderness.**'" (Exod. 14:10-12 NKJV) (Note: emphases in bold are my own.)

The people were not handling the situation well. Like most people do when they hit a roadblock, they thought about the good old days. The past became more glamorous and prosperous than it was.

How can these people, just freed from slavery, say that it would be better to die as slaves so they would get a proper burial? Who does a proper burial: the living or the dead? They were not only thinking of a proper burial; they were reminding Moses that they had told him the whole idea of freeing them would not work. Now was the proof; the Red Sea was before them, and the Egyptian army was on their heels, with no way for them to escape.

The people were right in thinking there was no way of escape for them because, humanly speaking, there was no way. The Egyptian army was furious and bloodthirsty. All the first-born children in Egypt had been killed by the angel of death because God was punishing them for not letting the Hebrews leave. They had been ordered by Pharaoh to bring the people back into slavery, because letting go of this free labor did not make sense.

Do you feel you have been pushed against the wall? You obeyed God and got married, and now things are going south. It seems everything is working against you, and there is no way for you to escape. Maybe you started a business with a lot of excitement because you were finally stepping into what you believed you were created to do. Everything started well but has taken a sudden turn for the worse. Your cash flow is negative, and your creditors are on your neck and threatening to take away all you have labored for the past couple of years.

It is not the time to panic; you have been prepared to overcome this obstacle or whatever challenge you may be facing. You must look closely at your situation, ensuring that you are correctly integrating the past into it. Your history has something to do with where you are going, and you should never neglect or discount your past experiences. You will fall into helplessness and hopelessness if you minimize where you have already been.

Let us see how Moses handled the situation, taking charge:

> "And Moses said to the people, 'Do not be afraid. Stand still, and see the salvation of the Lord, which He will accomplish for you today. For the Egyptians whom you see today, you shall see again no more forever. The Lord will fight for you, and you shall hold your peace.'
>
> And the Lord said to Moses, 'Why do you cry to Me? Tell the children of Israel to go forward. But lift up your rod and stretch out your hand over the sea and divide it. And the children of Israel shall go on dry ground through the midst of the sea." (Exod. 14:13-16 NKJV)

A couple of things come out of this passage, and we will be examining them separately to grasp these critical principles.

At Times, Doing Nothing is More Profitable

There are times when inaction is better than action. While it is difficult to be still in the face of uncertainty, turmoil, and attacks by the enemy, at times, this is what you must do to succeed.

That is precisely what Moses did. We are told Moses declared that the Israelites had to be still if they wanted to see God's deliverance. This was not an easy thing to do because the people were between a rock and a hard place. How could they be still when the Egyptian army was about to slaughter them? If they moved forward, they would drown in the Red Sea. In this situation, they could not just stand there, allowing the army to run over them.

At least the people could look for rocks and defend themselves or send a spokesperson to negotiate with the Egyptian military to spare their lives. Interestingly, Moses did not even ask them to fast and pray or do anything. He told them to be still!

It is challenging to be still amid difficulties. I remember how I lost more than $3500 in 2010 because I was trying to be still, but some of my close friends interpreted it as inaction. They kept pressuring me to do something to change my situation. You must have heard the expression, "Any action is better than no action."

I was being pressured to do something with my immigration situation because, at that time, I had been living in the US for almost a decade with no official work authorization. In 2010, I had lost my job, and it was impossible to get a new one because of a declining economy and lack of a work permit. Aside from all these, I was also enrolled in an MBA program; it was the only way I could legally stay in the country.

My friends were suggesting that I contact a lawyer and try to file papers for a green card. A part of me just wanted to wait and do nothing, but the pressure became unbearable, and I succumbed.

About a week after I had seen a lawyer and deposited $3500, the results of the DV Lottery came out, and I was selected to receive a green card. I immediately went back to the lawyers for a refund, but they refused. I learned a costly lesson.

King Saul Acted Rashly

If you think taking premature action is a light matter, think again. While many people are aware of King Saul's refusal to obey God's command to eliminate the Amalekites (and how this cost him the kingdom), it is also worth noting that Saul's troubles started way before he went to fight the Amalekites.

King Saul was impatient and could not be still. He could not see beyond the immediate pressure he felt. Just like the justification he gave for not slaughtering all the animals, he valued his men and their opinions more than God's.

Israel was brought to fight against the Philistines, and both armies gathered in Gilgal. A sacrifice had to be made by the prophet Samuel, one that would usher the people into battle. After waiting for a week for Samuel to show up and offer the sacrifice, there was no Samuel in sight. This did not sit well with King Saul, as some of his men were deserting him. King Saul became agitated, worried, and afraid. So, he took matters into his own hands and offered the sacrifice that was solely the responsibility of Samuel, the prophet.

It is written that as soon as he finished offering the sacrifice, the prophet Samuel showed up. Had King Saul waited one more day, he would have passed this crucial test. Sadly, King Saul failed this test, sealing his kingdom's fate.

Here is the exchange between King Saul and Samuel the prophet:

> "And Samuel said, 'What have you done?' Saul said, 'When I saw that the people were scattered from me, and that you did not come within the days appointed, and that the Philistines gathered together at Michmash, then I said, *The Philistines will now come down on me at Gilgal, and I have not made supplication to the Lord.* Therefore, I felt compelled, and offered a burnt offering.'
>
> And Samuel said to Saul, 'You have done foolishly. You have not kept the commandment of the Lord your God, which He commanded you. For now the Lord would have established your kingdom over Israel forever. But now your kingdom shall not continue. The Lord has sought for Himself a man after His own heart, and the Lord has commanded him to be commander over His people, because you have not kept what the Lord commanded you.'" (1 Sam. 13:11-14 NKJV)

Poor King Saul, he used words such as "I felt compelled" (1 Sam. 13:12 NKJV) to describe the pressure upon him. *Often people incorrectly believe that the end justifies the means.* According to them, what matters is good intentions, and then – everything goes. *If you want lasting success, understand that the end does not justify the means. What justifies your actions are unchanging principles and not just how you feel or what's popular and trending.*

King Saul saw the people deserting him, and he panicked and offered a sacrifice he was not supposed to provide. This situation called for inaction, and Saul failed the test. His failure cost him and his descendants the kingdom. Instead of a long-lasting kingdom, he became the first and only king from his tribe. Had he focused his attention on God – who had made him king – he would not have been moved when his troops were deserting him.

The take-home message: there is a time to be still, and you would be wise to be still when appropriate. For example, when a farmer plants seeds, he must remain still, waiting for the seeds to germinate, grow, and bear fruit. Any attempt to harvest before the crops mature will ruin everything. How many things in your life have been ruined because you could not stay still? There are times when it is best to keep quiet, saying nothing rather than speaking and inflaming the situation more.

Do Not Get Stuck in Your Past

While it is important to factor in the past, this should be done with wisdom. Change can be difficult. This explains why many like to maintain the status quo, the familiar, the predictable, and comfortable. The danger of maintaining the status quo is that it places limitations on you, preventing you from being versatile.

Before Moses encountered the Red Sea, the rod in his hand had been turned into a snake. That is all Moses knew the rod could do; it didn't occur to him that the rod had *other uses*. Making use of what you have will require thinking outside the box; each situation will be different, and you should be willing to adjust your strategy.

Someone once said: If every problem that you encounter is treated as a nail, then the only solution that you have will be to pound that nail with a hammer.

But life is more complicated than this. Therefore, what worked yesterday may not work today. This explains why we must operate on principles – not just emotions and trendy solutions.

Where there is an Obstacle, there is a Miracle

We often say that if you do not break the egg, you cannot have an omelet. If a seed does not die, it will not increase. While it may be painful for the seed to go through the dying process, it is in dying that the tree grows. The tree represents all the potential already stored in the seed.

When you come across any obstacles, there is a miracle waiting to happen. Without sickness, there is no healing. Without a need, there cannot be a supply. Darkness is the absence of light, and without darkness, we cannot appreciate the light.

Therefore, the presence of an obstacle or challenge indicates that a solution is also present. This is why we are often told not to be anxious, fearful, or worried. The admonition to not be afraid or worried would not make sense if there were no solution to whatever challenge or problem we may be facing. But the fact is, there is always a solution!

Never forget that you already have the solution to whatever you are facing. The little that you already have in your hand will become the miracle when you trust God with it.

The Problem Lies in How You See

This chapter has been talking about perception. While our physical eyes are essential for us to connect with the physical world, it is vital to learn how to see with the eyes of our minds. This is the type of seeing that enables us to make use of what we already have.

Without the ability to look beyond what our physical eyes take in, we would be stuck. The people cried out to Moses because all they saw was the Egyptian army and the Red Sea. They could not see the salvation of God. If they could have seen with their mind's eyes that God would deliver them, they would not have been so disturbed. Unfortunately, all they saw was the greatest army on Earth at their heels and the angry Red Sea waiting to drown them.

The people could not connect the dots to see that God, who had delivered them out of Egypt, could take them to the Promised Land. The more they focused on their physical circumstances, the more desperate they became, and finally, they cried out in anguish.

Your problem is not the obstacle or challenge you are facing right now; it is how you *perceive* it.

CHAPTER FOUR

Bad Things Happen to Good People

Perspective is everything because it determines how we interpret the things that happen to us. Evil is evil, and it will never be good. Light will never be darkness, and darkness will never be light. But light is the absence of darkness. *Without darkness, we cannot appreciate the light.* That said, light and darkness are not equal in strength. Therefore, no matter how dark a room is, when the light of a small candle is introduced, it displaces the darkness.

The presence of evil and bad things happening to good people has perplexed mankind for thousands of years, and that issue will not be resolved within the few pages of this book. But I do suggest a better way of looking at this issue of bad things happening to good people. Most of the time, when we think we have done everything right, we expect to be rewarded with the good things of life.

Part of the problem we run into when concluding that bad things have overtaken a good person is that the pain and suffering prevent us from seeing the bigger picture. There is always a picture that is bigger than the momentary suffering. I am not suggesting that someone who has lost their job is not feeling pain, and I'm not suggesting that someone who has lost a child is not going through anguish and distress. When someone suffers a loss, it is painful; they should be allowed to mourn and grieve.

But human nature expects (and at times, even *demands*) that when we do good, we should receive a good reward. This explains why, when evil suddenly strikes an individual who has been good all their lives, many people are perplexed. For example, someone who has never drank alcohol or smoked a cigarette is diagnosed with lung cancer and given a few months to live; most will wonder why such a thing happened.

Also, perplexing: when bad deeds are seemingly rewarded with good. Most expect to be rewarded with good when they do good; anything to the contrary does not sit well. We need not look far to see how a righteous act by Joseph landed him into prison. Joseph had refused to commit adultery with his master's wife, but she tried to force him. Joseph ran away from her, but she lied about it (a #MeToo moment that happened thousands of years ago). This woman fabricated a story against an innocent young man, and everybody believed her. Instead of being rewarded for not committing adultery, Joseph was thrown into jail with no possibility of parole or of ever being released. There was no trial, no defense lawyers, and no appeals court to represent him.

Are you in a situation right now where you feel that good things are supposed to be happening to you because, to the best of your ability, you have been good and have done everything right? Do you feel other people seem to get a break, even though they deserve to be punished for their bad deeds? Before you think that you have been singled out to be tortured, I want you to meet the wife of one of the prophets of old.

Again, you may wonder what the life of this woman that lived thousands of years ago has to do with your present predicament. Pay close attention, because if you are hurting right now and faced with an extremely difficult situation, you have more in common with this woman than you think.

Meet the Prophet's Widow

When people hear the word "prophet," they think of someone who has a close relationship with God, a person who has everything together, someone you wouldn't expect to be in any sort of need. Yet, we are about to meet the widow of a prophet, whose husband not only died penniless but did not leave anything for her. To make matters worse, the prophet was so poor he could not pay his debts before passing away.

It is unimaginable what this woman must have gone through. One may speculate that she was the talk of the city, and some people might have looked down on her with scorn because she was poor. Others might have judged her and her husband because, by being a prophet, he was supposed to lead by example. How could a man of God get into such debt, not even able to pay them off at his deathbed?

Who knows? Maybe he had a lousy spending attitude and would not listen to the advice of his wife. Instead, he kept digging the debt hole deeper and deeper, placing his family in a tight place financially. Today, many families are experiencing financial ruin because the husband insists that they must have that boat, car, vacation home, or whatever big-money item he must buy. This is an unfortunate situation that needs to be addressed. If you are that type of husband, it would be wise to get into some financial counseling before it becomes too late for you and your family.

I am not trying to bash husbands here. Perhaps the problem was the uncontrolled spending habits of this prophet's wife. She might have had a taste for expensive foods and fine clothes, and she was the one pushing her husband to keep borrowing to fuel her fancy lifestyle. If your husband has been complaining about your spending habits (and you have been resisting him, refusing to cut back), please, you need to do something about that. Money is hard to earn – spending is immensely easier – if you are not careful, you can dig a debt hole that proves difficult to dig yourself from. It's been said that you should stop spending money to buy things that you do not need because you are trying to impress people who do not care. If you can afford that designer bag, go for it, but to buy it just because you want to make an impression is the wrong motivation and it will keep you poor.

We'll end the speculations about what happened with this prophet of God who died broke and left nothing but debt for his family, and focus, instead, on the way forward. It does not matter what has been done in the past that has led you to where you are right now. The important thing is to keep moving forward.

Nothing will stop you if you do not allow it. As we are soon to discover, this widow had too many excuses and complaints and had her own ideas of what solution she needed, but there was a better way of which she was not aware. It would take a different person to help her refocus on what really mattered. I hope this book enables you to focus on the solution that has been with you all this time.

Seek Help in the Right Places

Many people choose the wrong solutions when they have difficulties. Some try to numb the pain in their lives by turning to drugs, alcohol abuse, and other destructive behaviors. Some of these remedies provide temporary relief but dig a deeper hole of despair, misery, and hopelessness because the void in their hearts cannot be numbed by such things. Some people, no longer able to bear it any longer, commit suicide. Unfortunately, these people use a permanent solution to solve a temporary problem. *Please – depression, anxiety,*

stress, and unhappiness can push you to the brink. If you are
struggling in any of these areas, it's essential that you look for
help.

The widow of the prophet did not go to rob a bank
or prostitute herself for money. She went to see the
prophet Elisha, perhaps because she was the wife of a
prophet; Elisha was the main prophet, and her husband
had worked under his leadership. Listen to her plea:

> "The wife of a man from the company of the
> prophets cried out to Elisha, 'Your servant my
> husband is dead, and you know that he revered
> the Lord. But now his creditor is coming to
> take my two boys as his slaves.'" (2 Kings 4:1)

When this widow went before the prophet, she did not
hide her problem and did not attempt to sugarcoat it.
She cried out in pain and anguish because she was in
need and sought help. Some are in distress and need
help but are too proud to ask for it, justifying their
stance by saying they don't want to be a burden to
anybody. This type of prideful attitude has led many
people to their doom. It is okay to ask for help; none
of us are sufficient in ourselves – we were created for
relationships. Remember: whatever gifts you have are
meant to serve other people, not just yourself. Of
course, you'll take care of yourself, but taking care of
others implies that you have cared for yourself first.

The widow dealt with the issue of "why bad things
happen to good people" because she reminded the
prophet that her husband loved her and was faithful.

Yet he died in debt, and her children were about to be taken away and turned into slaves. This was a double-whammy for this poor widow. Her dead husband had not only left her penniless, but the debt they owed would also cause their children to be sold into slavery.

Know What You Need – and What You Don't

As simple as this may appear, it is not easy to know what you need, as the case of this woman demonstrates. She was so overwhelmed by her debt and the possibility of her sons becoming slaves that she became desperate. But the prophet wanted to know:

> "Elisha replied to her, 'How can I help you? Tell me, what do you have in your house?' 'Your servant has nothing there at all,' she said, 'except a small jar of olive oil.'" (2 Kings 4:2)

This widow must have thought that when the prophet heard about her pathetic situation, he would give her money to pay off the debts she owed. There is no indication whatsoever that she was hoping to participate in solving her debt problem. The two questions Elisha asked seemed out of place.

How could the prophet be asking *what she had* after she had just told him that her husband had died, leaving them destitute and her sons to be sold into slavery? Was the prophet deaf? She needed *money* to solve her problem.

There is much power in confession; the power of life and death lies in our tongue. When you are in a tough situation, you must learn how to articulate well in terms of what's going on.

Secondly, it is written, "Ask and it shall be given to you." (Matt. 7:7) If you ask, you will receive. This implies that if you do not ask, you will not receive. The prophet wanted the widow to move from complaining to asking. While she had poured out her problem, she hadn't stated precisely what she needed.

Permit me to take a little detour here. In marriage, often the women expect their husbands to do certain things they haven't explicitly asked. Wives may assume that their spouse has been around long enough and should know what they need – and just do it. Husbands often become frustrated and perplexed; if the wife would just remind them and state clearly what they want, married life would be much easier.

But the wife wants the husband to read their minds and deliver. This is a recipe for disaster and has caused a lot of pain in marriages. If you're expecting your husband to read your mind, you're inviting frustration, and nagging will just make things worse. To receive, you must ask, even if you've been married for over thirty years!

You must know precisely what you need so that when asked, you can articulate it well. For instance, if you go to the doctor with an illness and the wrong medication is prescribed, your condition will not improve.

You should not take this issue lightly. Even Jesus Christ required clarity before he healed blind Bartimaeus, as this conversation between them illustrates:

"Now they came to Jericho. As He went out of Jericho with His disciples and a great multitude, blind Bartimaeus, the son of Timaeus, sat by the road begging. And when he heard that it was Jesus of Nazareth, he began to cry out and say, 'Jesus, Son of David, have mercy on me!' Then many warned him to be quiet; but he cried out all the more, 'Son of David, have mercy on me!' So, Jesus stood still and commanded him to be called. Then they called the blind man, saying to him, 'Be of good cheer. Rise, He is calling you.' And throwing aside his garment, he rose and came to Jesus. So, Jesus answered and said to him,

'What do you want Me to do for you?' The blind man said to Him, 'Rabboni, that I may receive my sight.' Then Jesus said to him, 'Go your way; your faith has made you well.' And immediately he received his sight and followed Jesus on the road." (Mark 10:46-52 NKJV)

Can you imagine how this blind man felt when he cried out for mercy, and Jesus showed up and asked him what he wanted? The man was obviously blind; one would have expected Jesus to go ahead and just heal the man, but he did not heal him immediately. Just like the prophet Elisha asked the woman, "How can I help you?" (2 Kings 4:2) Jesus asked, "What do you want Me to do for you?" (Mark 10:51) The man had to open his mouth and ask what he wanted Jesus Christ to do for him, even though everybody knew that he was blind.

The blind man asked for mercy, but he needed more than mercy; he needed to see. Thank God he did not get angry when Jesus asked him what he needed. Do you know what you need? Can you articulate it precisely? Have you asked for help?

Let's return to the widow. The next question Elisha asked the widow was even more perplexing: "Tell me, what do you have in your house?" (2 Kings 4:2) Poor widow, she was hurting and in need of immediate relief, and all she received were questions. Now they asked if she had something at home.

What is going on? Did the prophet not realize that she wouldn't be there in the first place if she had something? This explains why her first response was, "Your servant has nothing there at all." (2 Kings 4:2) She believed that she had nothing, and that is why she came to the prophet in the first place.

I cannot imagine what was running through this poor widow's mind as she searched for answers to the questions being thrown at her. She had come for a solution, and now she was being placed in an uncomfortable situation. She just said she had nothing because it should be evident to the prophet that she had nothing. Then she remembered that she had a little oil.

The Power in a Little

What the prophet said next must have perplexed her further. He did not give the money that she needed but gave her these instructions:

> "Elisha said, 'Go around and ask all your neighbors for empty jars. Don't ask for just a few. Then go inside and shut the door behind you and your sons. Pour oil into all the jars, and as each is filled, put it to one side.' She left him and shut the door behind her and her sons. They brought the jars to her and she kept pouring. When all the jars were full, she said to her son, 'Bring me another one.' But he replied, 'There is not a jar left.' Then the oil stopped flowing. She told the man of God, and he said, 'Go, sell the oil and pay your debts. You and your sons can live on what is left.'" (2 Kings 4:3-7)

I must commend this woman for her obedience. She came with a problem, but an unlikely solution was given to her, yet she did not complain. It is incredible that she went ahead and followed the instructions given to her.

Another Widow Who Experienced an Abundance

There is a lot of lack and poverty in the world today; many barely have enough to eat, leaving them malnourished. Can you imagine living on less than a dollar a day? While the reasons behind poverty are complicated (and solutions not easily applicable), we cannot throw up our hands, giving up because of the enormity of the problem.

In most cases, while charity is mostly geared at relieving the symptoms of the problem (without sustainability in mind), it is more productive to focus on getting to the root of the problem. This requires some heavy lifting, equipping, and empowerment that must integrate with what people already have. Self-worth and dignity are restored when they are empowered to make use of what they already possess; giving handouts without empowering and equipping them to take ownership is not a good idea.

Let me introduce you to another widow who was about to starve to death through no fault of her own. She and her son were on their last leg and just waiting for the inevitable to happen. They were preparing to starve to death when the prophet Elijah showed up.

Before Elijah showed up, he had been fed by ravens for some time, and the supply ran out. Then God sent him to a poor widow in Sidon. It makes one wonder: were there no widows in Israel? Yes, there likely were, but

God sent Elijah to a *foreign country*, not to a rich person, but to a widow who barely had anything. At times you may find yourself in strange places with an assignment that you think you are entirely ill-equipped to handle based on your circumstances.

But if God has sent you, provision has already been made, and all you need to do is take a close look at what you already have and let God take care of the rest.

Can you imagine how crazy it was for Elijah to depend on birds for his nourishment? What if they didn't show up? What if someone killed them? As strange as this may sound, Elijah depended on these birds for a while and did not go hungry; eventually, though, the brook dried up, and he had to move on.

Unexpected Encounters

The widow in our story was not expecting to meet Elijah. Instead, she was going about her day-to-day activities, when suddenly she met this strange man, making some very unusual requests.

> "Then the word of the Lord came to him, saying, 'Arise, go to Zarephath, which belongs to Sidon, and dwell there. See, I have commanded a widow there to provide for you.' So he arose and went to Zarephath. And when he came to the gate of the city, indeed, a widow was there gathering sticks. And he called to her and said, 'Please bring me a little water in a cup,

that I may drink.' And as she was going to get it, he called to her and said, 'Please bring me a morsel of bread in your hand.'" (1 Kings 17:8-11 NKJV)

The prophet Elijah was hungry when he met this widow; asking for food from her was not a symbolic gesture. He needed it, as his supplies had run out. It appeared as if he might be in the wrong place because the woman was in pretty bad shape, to say the least:

"So she said, 'As the Lord your God lives, I do not have bread, only a handful of flour in a bin, and a little oil in a jar; and see, I am gathering a couple of sticks that I may go in and prepare it for myself and my son, that we may eat it, and die.'" (1 Kings 17:12 NKJV)

This widow gave the typical response given by many. She focused on the obstacle she was facing, then moved on to complaining and self-pity. The more she painted how dire her situation was, the bleaker the situation became. She started from *I do not have any bread* and ended with *death*. Her condition went downhill immediately; she said she had nothing.

What we focus on tends to become magnified, taking on a life of its own. Therefore, it is essential to focus on solutions and not just the problems you may be facing. While the natural tendency is to focus on the problems (leading others to show sympathy), sadly, the situation is made worse.

"And Elijah said to her, 'Do not fear; go and do as you have said, but make me a small cake from it first, and bring it to me, and afterward make some for yourself and your son. For thus says the Lord God of Israel: "The bin of flour shall not be used up, nor shall the jar of oil run dry, until the day the Lord sends rain on the earth."' So she went away and did according to the word of Elijah, and she and he and her household ate for many days. The bin of flour was not used up, nor did the jar of oil run dry, according to the word of the Lord which He spoke by Elijah." (1 Kings 17:13-16 NKJV)

Let's Meet Another Widow

Many people are waiting for the day they'll have plenty of money before they start investing, but time is passing by and working against them. Some others are waiting for the day when they will have enough time to prioritize their health by exercising regularly.

Unfortunately for them, each passing day works against them. There is no neutral place in terms of time. Your health is either improving or deteriorating. Many other people do not give to charity or other people in need because they are waiting for the day when they will have enough to spare. The problem is that this is a heart issue and not that of lack; many people expand their expenses when their incomes increase, leaving them with little to give to others. Some have not started their business because they are waiting for a lot of capital to start. You should stop waiting for plentifulness because there is power in the small amount that you already have.

You Must Follow Instructions

The instructions that the prophet gave to this widow did not make sense. One would have expected the prophet to provide her with a money bag to immediately pay her debts, but all she got were some "silly" instructions to borrow containers and start pouring the little oil into them. There is even a ridiculous request that she close the door of the house before filling up the containers; she needed money to pay her creditors and not some exercise in futility! How would completing these thoughtless, no-good, and unscientific instructions help this widow? The list of questions and objections has no end, but the widow did the smart thing by following the instructions. She understood that if she did not follow them, her situation would not change.

Follow Instructions, Save Your Marriage

The statistics are stacked against marriages these days; about fifty percent of all marriages in the US end in divorce. This implies that if you are already married or planning to get married, the odds are against you.

A fifty percent divorce rate is exceptionally high: out of every ten marriages, about five ends in divorce. While many people downplay the harmful and terrible effects of divorce, it should not be treated lightly. The hurt, trauma, and destruction that accompanies divorce can

– and should be – avoided by all. But many people do not know what they already have, do not use it, and stubbornly refuse to follow instructions.

Many marriages have ended in divorce because both husband and wife have refused to follow instructions. The words "I am sorry" are some of the most challenging words in the English language. Some couples would rather let their marriage break down than to say, "I am sorry." Their pride and insistence on being right are more important than their marriage. Other couples will say that being right is not more important than their marriage, but their actions speak louder than words.

Unfortunately, the instructions of a marriage counselor do not make sense to couples who insist on doing it their way. They still wonder why their marriage is on the rocks and about to break. Some are waiting for a "miracle" to happen. According to them, things will just fix themselves and work out – even if they do nothing.

While some couples agree to do something to improve the situation, they decide to do it their own way. The instructions of the counselor do not make sense to them, and in their minds, they know better than the experts.

Consider the following powerful statement Albert Einstein made: "The significant problems we face cannot be solved at the same level of thinking we were at when we created them." In other words, you need to make some changes if you want to dig yourself out of whatever hole you may be in right now.

Why is this common sense neglected by so many, to their own peril? If you are married, why would you continue to get advice on how to handle issues in your marriage from unmarried people? What do you expect them to tell you? Head knowledge always makes sense, but experiential knowledge brings life. If someone has never been married (or if they've been married, but are now divorced), be careful of their advice. While these individuals may have no malice in their hearts, their counsel may be misleading – or dead wrong.

There is a big difference between head knowledge and experiential knowledge. If head knowledge were all that we needed for our marriages to succeed, the fifty percent divorce rate we're currently experiencing would disappear.

Many people have the *head knowledge* that it is not healthy to commit adultery, yet they do it anyway. Some "know" lying to each other is not healthy for their marriage, but they lie nevertheless. Others "know" that a gentle answer turns away wrath and that constant nagging will ruin their marriage, yet they yell, scream, and nag. It is common wisdom that women should not use sex as a weapon against their husbands, but women deprive their husbands of this marital privilege when they are angry. The list of things husbands and wives should not do can go on and on; many can talk about these rules, yet their actions speak differently.

The last thing couples must take into serious consideration – if they want a robust, lasting marriage – is to make sure they do not take each other for granted. It's easy to do. You may think some action or behavior is expected; therefore, it should not be appreciated. To make use of what's already going well in your marriage, you must appreciate each other daily.

Why not make it a practice to thank your spouse at the end of each day for one or two good things they did for you? Take some time and look into your husband's or wife's eyes and thank them from the bottom of your heart. Is it asking too much for you to appreciate your wife for the meal she prepared for you? These little acts can help save your marriage and prevent it from ending up in divorce.

Above all, read good marriage books and ensure that you follow the instructions in these books. It is better to read one book and follow the instructions than to read a hundred and do nothing with the information. Too many claim to know the secret to a happy marriage, articulating what they *say they know* exceptionally well. But they do not act on this information. No wonder many marriages are suffering; some are stunted, and many are dying.

Make use of what you already have – the information you have about building solid marriages – before you ask for more information or attend another marriage seminar. You will be wise in doing this; it will make your marriage grow stronger and prevent it from deteriorating and breaking down.

Follow Instructions; It Will Improve Your Health

Your health is ground zero because, without good health, nothing else matters. Many people think that they can afford to gamble with their health, but this is, unfortunately, one area in which it is impossible to succeed while cheating or taking shortcuts.

Food is the avenue through which our bodies receive nourishment for proper functioning and sustenance. This implies that we must pay close attention to what, when, why, and even *where* we eat. While the debate regarding the relationship between nutrition and medicine rages on, we cannot deny that obesity is on the rise globally, and heart disease has become the number-one killer in the US. Similar trends in the increase of heart disease are observed in countries that have adopted the western diet.

These days, many people rely on the fast-food industry because it is convenient and easily accessible. But is this food healthy for the body? Of what use is drinking sugar, mixed with CO_2 and some color and artificial flavors?

While there is no point in becoming the food police, people must take individual responsibility to control what goes into their mouths. Whatever you eat must be processed by your body. If you put junk into your body, it will negatively affect your health.

When you visit communities that do not have processed foods and eat food harvested directly from the farm to the pot, you can see significant differences in their body mass index. These people are often leaner and have less prevalence of obesity. There are some in the medical community who push back on any idea that food can be an integral part of maintaining proper health. This is unfortunate because, at the end of the day, it is better to be healthy and have no need for medication than to be on ten-plus different drugs. While pharmacology has increasingly played a central role in modern medicine (and helped to save many lives), it is essential not to forget the side effects of some of these medications.

You must do all that is within your power to prevent yourself from being in a situation where you need medication. Eating fewer sugary, processed foods will help you stay healthy. Too much animal protein, while popular, is not suitable for you, and it is in your best interest to cut back on such products. There are always alternatives, and you should consider eating those.

Another thing to consider is portion size. Using food as a source of comfort can become a problem when you eat more than your body can use. Some turn to food when they are stressed or depressed, eating more than their bodies can burn, resulting in weight gain.

The more they eat, the more weight they put on, and the more they gain weight, the more unhappy they become. As you can see, it is easy to fall into a vicious cycle that becomes almost impossible to break.

The other major part of health and wellness is exercise. You cannot continue eating more calories than you are using and not expect to put on weight. If you are not exercising regularly and consistently, you are doing yourself a disservice. While we may argue all day about the benefits of moderate exercise, do it and see for yourself how much your health improves! Before you wait for the results to be peer-reviewed and sanctioned by science, as some are claiming, go out three times a week and exercise for at least thirty minutes. The benefits will make you a believer.

Many people use strange excuses to justify why they are unwilling to give up the bad, destructive habits that are killing them. Not too long ago, we discussed health, fitness, and wellness, and someone said that their grandmother smoked all her life and lived to be more than eighty years old. Therefore, they argued, spending time exercising and watching what you eat is a waste of time because we will all die.

What this person fails to understand is that just because their grandmother smoked and did not get lung cancer, there is no guarantee that another person can do the same and have similar results. Over the years, studies have established a strong link between smoking and lung cancer and other forms of cancer. Therefore, it is wise to stop smoking because it reduces the probability of getting the type of cancers linked to smoking.

Other people say that the state of their health results from their family history or genetics. In other words, everybody in their family has a history of being overweight and diabetes-prone. What these individuals avoid considering is the eating and health habits of their families.

The issue may be tied directly to a poor diet that, if improved, can break this history of disease, suffering, and untimely deaths. This has severe consequences that you readily witness when you meet people whose legs, hands, and other body parts have been amputated because of diabetes.

The choice is yours. Reading about nutrition, health, fitness, and wellness is something that everybody should do. When you read and find essential instructions, you should follow them. It is only when you follow the instructions that you will reap the results of good health.

Start with what you have. Many people do not exercise because they think they need specialized equipment, but the truth is that you do not need any fancy exercise products or gym memberships. If you have two legs, you can go out and walk and run. Make use of what you already have and stop giving excuses for not doing what you ought to be doing.

Follow Instructions; It Will Increase Your Wealth

Many people dream of the day they will become rich so they can have enough money to start investing it. Many have kept waiting and waiting, and now it is too late because, for money to grow, *you need time*. When you do not have time on your side, it is difficult to build wealth. The best time to plant a tree was yesterday. Likewise, the best time to start investing was yesterday.

While there is nothing wrong with having grand dreams, it is vital to learn how the process works. If you keep waiting for the perfect time to start saving money, you'll never begin; *there is no perfect time*. If you don't create a savings plan and stick to it, nothing will happen; each dollar that you earn will be pulled in many different directions. The lure to spend is stronger than the desire to save. You must have a game plan.

Do you know that you are supposed to pay yourself first before you pay other people? So, why do you work year-in and year-out, never paying yourself? How much do you think you are supposed to pay yourself out of all the money you work hard to earn? Many simply don't understand that they deserve to be paid first, let alone consider the amount.

From each dollar earned today, about twenty cents should be reserved for when the time comes that you no longer have the strength to work – as you do now. It's wise to save money for that time, as well as for rainy days.

This issue of saving for rainy days and winter months prompted King Solomon to say:

> "Go to the ant, you sluggard!
> Consider her ways and be wise,
> Which, having no captain,
> Overseer or ruler,
> Provides her supplies in the summer,
> And gathers her food in the harvest.
> How long will you slumber, O sluggard?
> When will you rise from your sleep?
> A little sleep, a little slumber,
> A little folding of the hands to sleep—
> So shall your poverty come on you like a prowler,
> And your need like an armed man." (Prov. 6:6-11 NKJV)

Interestingly, the wisest person who ever lived instructs us to learn from the tiny, lowly ants. He has the authority to do so because if tiny ants have figured out how to store food for winter, humans (who are smarter on all counts than the ants) should know better. One would assume that people know to do this, but the sad reality is that many people live beyond their means, going into debt.

We are in the midst of an instant gratification generation where "if you want it, you can have it" – right now. The question of affordability does not come up, because of the availability and easy access to credit. Many people choose to buy now and pay later. By the time they finish paying for what they just bought, there's a newer version available, and they decide to buy on credit again and again. This constant pursuit of material things precludes any savings, let alone investments to grow that money.

While common sense demands you do not spend more than you earn, many people feel they can outsmart this simple system. They overstretch their finances and are cash strapped all the time, keeping them from taking advantage of investment opportunities when they arise. No wonder such people continue to be poor and broke!

Without investing your money (that which was saved), putting it to work for you, it's impossible to reap profit or become financially independent. Instead, money is spent on "stuff" – some of which you may need, but much of which you could do without.

Sadly, too many are concerned with impressing others because they are insecure inside. These individuals seldom agree that they lack inner self-assurance, arguing and defending their consumption with every fiber of their being. They feel they are just "keeping up with the times," unwilling to be left behind or not fit in.

While these excuses appear to make some sense superficially, a close look reveals that people are using them to mask their insecurities and justify their unscrupulous consumption.

Your hard-earned money should be put to work for you, not used to buy things you do not need because you want to impress people who do not care. You may be under the impression that those you are trying to impress notice you and care; you're wrong, they don't!

Therefore, focus on saving your money and letting it grow for you – you'll likely need it in the future. The temptation to buy things is real, and you must resist it. Remember, it isn't the amount of money you make that matters, but what you *do with* the money you earn.

Lastly, while it may appear that making more money will make saving easier, you probably underestimate (or be taken unawares by) the demands made on the extra money earned. Your car may suddenly need upgrading, and your home may need remodeling, etc. You may take that vacation you have been putting off for so long. In short, many things will show up and make demands on the extra money you earn.

Therefore, the smartest thing to do is start saving from what you already have now; it doesn't matter how small, but twenty percent of what you make belongs to you. When you have a moment, you can invest it, but be sure to consult with a financial professional.

Follow Instructions; It Will Give You Eternal Life

Life does not end when you die. There is an afterlife, and I am going to use this opportunity to tell you about it. Talking about the afterlife is not an indirect way for you to disengage with the present life, but a motivation to make the most of your time on Earth. While there are many arguments about which road leads to God and which of the "gods" is the true one, I will not dwell on these issues – there is not enough room for us to do a comparative study of world religions.

However, it is essential to note that while popular culture classifies Christianity as a religion (and tries to compare it to other religions), Christianity is *not a religion*. Religion is mankind trying their best to reach out to God and please Him. Christianity is the exact opposite, as God reaches out to mankind, doing all He can to redeem us. To enjoy this redemption God is offering, you must follow instructions.

I am writing this with the assumption that you have been reconciled with God and have a relationship with Him. If you do not yet have a relationship with God, I will give you the opportunity here to take care of that. This is one of the most important decisions you will ever make and should not take it lightly. I do not want you to allow the failures of other believers to prevent you from experiencing a personal relationship with your Heavenly Father. He has been waiting for you to come home and be reunited with Him.

Here is your opportunity to come home to the fullness of life, abundant life. All that you need and desire is in God, and you will never be forsaken or abandoned.

Let me start by asking you the following question. Do you have a personal relationship with Jesus Christ? This question is being asked because, although all roads lead to Rome, not all roads lead to the God of the Bible. Jesus Christ, who is God Incarnate, made some exclusive claims:

> "Jesus answered, 'I am the way and the truth and the life. No one comes to the Father except through me." (John 14:6)

This is a bold claim, and Jesus Christ died standing up for it. He is simply saying that if you want a relationship with the God of the Bible, the creator of heaven and earth, you must pass through Him. If you are not yet a follower of Jesus Christ, here is your opportunity to do so. I suggest this because it will get you connected to the source of all things, becoming spiritually alive, and living forever in God's presence. Raising your child in fear of God is the best thing you can do for yourself and your child.

The first and most important thing to understand is that we have all sinned. In other words, we cannot meet God's perfect standard, no matter how hard we try. Have you tried on your own to be good and realized many times you fail to measure up? Do you struggle with a void in your heart that nothing has been able to fill, no matter how hard you have tried? Are you comparing yourself to others and feeling that you are good because you are better than other people? If you answered yes to any of these questions, you need to understand that all of us have sinned, just as the following scriptures spell out:

"For all have sinned, and come short of the glory of God." (Rom. 3:23 King James Bible)

"For there is not a just man upon earth, that doeth good, and sinneth not." (Eccles. 7:20 KJB)

"But we are all as an unclean thing, and all our righteousnesses are as filthy rags, and we all do fade as a leaf; and our iniquities, like the wind, have taken us away." (Isa. 64:6 KJB)

"As it is written, There is none righteous, no, not one." (Rom. 3:10 KJB)

"For whosoever shall keep the whole law, and yet offend in one point, he is guilty of all." (James 2:10 KJB)

"If we say that we have no sin, we deceive ourselves, and the truth is not in us." (1 John 1:8 KJB)

We have all sinned and need God's forgiveness. This is the place to start. When you acknowledge this, then you can receive God's free forgiveness and salvation.

The third crucial thing to understand is the devastating consequences of sin. You may be wondering why sin is such a bad thing and why we are making such a big deal about it. Everyone – including you – should be concerned about the consequences of sin because, according to the following verse, sin has a wage, and that wage is death:

"For the wages of sin is death, but the free gift of God is eternal life in Christ Jesus our Lord." (Rom. 6:23 English Standard Version)

"Therefore, just as sin came into the world through one man, and death through sin, and so death spread to all men because all sinned" (Rom. 5:12 ESV)

"But as for the cowardly, the faithless, the detestable, as for murderers, the sexually immoral, sorcerers, idolaters, and all liars, their portion will be in the lake that burns with fire and sulfur, which is the second death." (Rev. 21:8 ESV)

This death is both physical and spiritual. Sin can cause us to die in this life, and if we die in sin, we will be separated from God forever. You do not want this to happen to you, your child, or children. You want to live forever in the presence of God (and this why the second crucial thing to think about is the wages of sin.)

The fourth crucial step is to ask God to forgive our sins. The good news is that God has already made provision for that, and is ready and willing to forgive us all our sins. As you will soon discover, God has already made the first move:

"For God so loved the world that He gave His only begotten Son, that whoever believes in Him should not perish but have everlasting life." (John 3:16 NKJV)

"Jesus said unto her, I am the resurrection, and the life: he that believeth in me, though he were dead, yet shall he live: And whosoever liveth and believeth in me shall never die. Believest thou this?" (John 11:25-26 KJB)

"And they said, Believe on the Lord Jesus Christ, and thou shalt be saved, and thy house." (Acts 16:31 KJB)

"That if thou shalt confess with thy mouth the Lord Jesus, and shalt believe in thine heart that God hath raised Him from the dead, thou shalt be saved. For with the heart man believeth unto righteousness; and with the mouth confession is made unto salvation." (Rom. 10:9-10 KJB)

"Whosoever believeth that Jesus is the Christ is born of God: and every one that loveth Him that begat loveth Him also that is begotten of Him." (1 John 5:1 KJB)

Now that you have confessed and asked Jesus to forgive your sins, your sins have been forgiven and will be remembered no more.

The fifth and final step is inviting Jesus into your heart. Now is your opportunity to surrender your life to Jesus and invite Him to come and live inside of you. Jesus will never force Himself on anyone. He is outside, according to the following scripture, knocking and waiting for you to invite Him in:

"Behold, I stand at the door, and knock: if any man hear my voice, and open the door, I will come in to him, and will sup with him, and he with me." (Rev. 3:20 KJB)

"But as many as received him, to them gave he power to become the sons of God, even to them that believe on his name:" (John 1:12 KJB)

"And because ye are sons, God hath sent forth the Spirit of his Son into your hearts, crying, Abba, Father." (Gal. 4:6 KJB)

"That Christ may dwell in your hearts by faith; that ye, being rooted and grounded in love," (Eph. 3:17 KJB)

Jesus Christ is waiting for you to invite Him to come in; pray, ask Him in your own words, or use the following prayer:

The Sinners Prayer (by John Barnett)

The following prayer expresses the desire to transfer trust to Christ alone for eternal salvation. If these words speak of your own heart's desire, praying them can be the link that will connect you to God.

"Dear God, I know that I am a sinner and there is nothing that I can do to save myself. I confess my complete helplessness to forgive my own sin or to work my way to heaven. At

> this moment I trust Christ alone as the One who bore my sin when He died on the cross. I believe that He did all that will ever be necessary for me to stand in your holy presence. I thank you that Christ was raised from the dead as a guarantee of my own resurrection. As best as I can, I now transfer my trust to Him. I am grateful that He has promised to receive me despite my many sins and failures. Father, I take you at your word. I thank you that I can face death now that you are my Savior. Thank you for the assurance that you will walk with me through the deep valley. Thank you for hearing this prayer. In Jesus' Name. Amen."

Praise God, Hallelujah! If you just said this prayer, I am super excited for you and want to use this opportunity to welcome you into the kingdom of God and God's family. This is one of the most important decisions you will ever make because it has eternal consequences. You are now a newborn baby in Christ and need spiritual nourishment to grow in your faith. If you need more information on what to do next, send an email.

Take time to understand the crucial nature of the decision you have just made. My focus has not been on you joining a religion or becoming religious. Religion is a man seeking to please God. But here we have presented a picture of God seeking man. God loved the entire world, then gave His son to pay the penalty for our sins. You are being called into a personal relationship with Jesus – not being called for some religious observances. While church membership is important, it is more important to establish a strong and vibrant relationship with Jesus Christ. (This entire plan of salvation has been borrowed from my material in other works; I have written it with a few modifications.)

To See the Miracle, You Need to Take the First Step

If you have sky-dived before, you will understand what I am about to say: without jumping out of the airplane, your parachute will never open. It doesn't matter what you think or how much you want the parachute to function; it won't, as long as you sit in the airplane and refuse to jump. Even when you jump, the parachute is not going to open immediately; instead, you experience some free fall. This is scary, to say the least, but you must trust the person who packed your parachute, believing that it will open at the critical moment.

I'm in no way suggesting that you take the first step without thinking carefully about the next one, but there's no point in allowing fear to prevent you from moving forward. Many people mask their fear by hiding behind "strategic planning." Do you think we would have airplanes today if the Wright Brothers spent all their time planning and perfecting their planes but never testing them? What about the thousand other inventions we enjoy today? These inventions would never have seen the light of day if they weren't tested.

No matter how well you plan and how meticulous your plans are, you will only know by taking the first step. Without the first step, there is no second step, let alone a third step, fourth step, etc. Sadly, many won't take that first step because it is the scariest and most challenging one.

What is holding you back from taking that first step towards becoming all you were created to be?

In 2001, I had the revelation that I should move to the US for graduate school; what I *didn't have* was the money or scholarship to do so. Still, I took the initial action of asking for an admission package from the University of Texas at Dallas, even though I knew that it was impossible for my family to raise the millions I thought was needed to get a graduate degree in the US.

I shared my dream with many, and a lot of them thought I'd lost my mind. Still, my only option was to step out in faith, an action that would eventually bring me to the US for graduate school. Then I packed my single suitcase, traveling over 8000 miles from my country of birth – without money or a scholarship.

I did not allow my fears to stop me. If you *don't try*, you have a hundred percent failure rate because, when you make an attempt, you have dramatically increased your chances of succeeding. This is precisely what I did, and I was able to secure admission, borrow funds to cover my airfare and show up in the US ready to study, with enough tuition work and money to pay for my room and board. And I experienced one miracle after another. I procured a teaching assistantship, eventually graduating with my doctorate in geosciences, debt-free. All my fears and worries melted away, and things worked out because I trusted God and took the first step.

Are you willing to take the first step towards a healthier you? Then start exercising today. Stop waiting for the perfect moment because it will never come. If there were an ideal moment, you would have taken advantage of it a long time ago. The only way to fight procrastination is by taking action. Perhaps you don't *feel like* working out and eating right. Your feelings should not be in charge; you are in charge and can exercise and eat right, so take responsibility ("respond to the ability") for your health.

Start with the little time you already have, and you will be amazed at how many doors will open for you. The two widows (and many people who have experienced supernatural growth and profoundly impacted others' lives) followed instructions and took the first step. The rest is history.

Stop waiting and start doing! Without action, you will not get what you are desiring, hoping, and praying. When you take the first step, all that you need will be delivered to you without fail.

CHAPTER FIVE

If Not You, Who Else?

When things are not going well or when disaster strikes, many people ask, "Why me?" This question may be followed by, "What have I done wrong?" There is nothing wrong with asking questions, especially when things happen in your life that make no sense. We must keep hope alive by training ourselves to see the bigger picture. This does not justify validating evil nor minimize the pain.

I just received a message on WhatsApp from a group belonging to my secondary school mates. This message is about the recent death of a seven-year-old girl who succumbed to kidney disease. Her case went viral because she didn't have the money for dialysis, but someone posted her story online; the money poured in, but it came too late. Why would a young child like her be afflicted with kidney disease? I can't imagine the anguish her family is enduring right now – the pain is real and should not be minimized.

As I write, there is an armed conflict in Cameroon (my country of birth) that has killed thousands, and thousands more have been displaced. Each day we receive gruesome pictures of beheadings and other atrocities. On a more personal note, my older sister's son got shot a few months ago, and my parents are now refugees. My father is on retirement and has been forced to flee his retirement home and live in the capital city. I am having a hard time processing this traumatic and challenging experience, and don't understand how they are handling it.

This week, Ethiopian Airlines flight 302 (on a four-month-old Boeing 737 Max 8) took off in Addis Ababa headed for Nairobi, Kenya, crashing just six minutes after takeoff. All 157 passengers and crew died. None of these people expected to die on this fateful day, nor were their families and loved ones prepared for such a tragedy. While investigations are ongoing, the families of those killed in this accident will forever be scarred by this tragic event.

This is just an inkling of the tragedies playing out all around us. Let's focus on how to keep moving when situations out of our hands are placing hurdles in our path. This is why asking the question, "Why me?" should be changed to, "If not me, who else?" "*Why me?*" takes us to a place of hopelessness, as its deeper meaning is that we don't deserve to have it happen to us. It feels unfair.

It isn't easy to take a slice of time from life, appreciating all that's going on, without factoring in the past, present, and future. Sadly, it's almost impossible to factor in the future; it's not here yet! We can all see the past (hindsight is 20/20), but in the midst of calamity, all you see is the devastation or obstacle before you. Consider how the fiancée of one of the people killed on the ill-fated Ethiopian Airlines flight 302 may be feeling right now. Her beloved was flying to Kenya to attend his mother's funeral, but he never made it. How will this man's fiancée handle this situation? I cannot imagine the heartache and trauma she – and all the other people who lost loved ones – are going through.

No matter what you are facing, asking "Why me?" may make momentary sense, but in the long run, it only leads to more confusion and hopelessness.

This book's message is centered on using what you already have to be successful in your life. We'll all face different challenges and temptations, experiencing victories and setbacks, and while most of us do well with successes, things get quickly out of hand when disaster strikes.

Therefore, it is crucial to learn how to navigate through the good, the bad, and the ugly. So far, all the examples we have seen involve people who used what they already had to solve challenges in their lives.

The following admonishment was given because we are human and still live on Earth. The temptation that comes our way has only one mission: our destruction. We should not allow this to happen, because:

> "No temptation has overtaken you except such as is common to man; but God is faithful, who will not allow you to be tempted beyond what you are able, but with the temptation will also make the way of escape, that you may be able to bear it." (1 Cor. 10:13 NKJV)

There is a way of escape from whatever is trying to make you live a life of regret, self-pity, and vengeance. To think otherwise is the worst thing you can do to yourself. You are *not* at the mercy of whatever is happening in your life right now; there is hope in Jesus Christ because He has promised to make a way of escape no matter how bad the situation. Change your focus from the enormity of the problem to the possibility of a way out.

Also, keep in mind that there are benefits in the trial or tribulation you are going through. Good can come out of this situation!

The best way to illustrate this is the story of Good Friday. When I was a child, it baffled me that the day Jesus Christ was brutally murdered is considered a special day. I wondered what good there was in the Son of God being accused and crucified for a crime He did not commit.

Some people may think Jesus, being God Incarnate, didn't suffer on the cross, but instead just put on a show. No, he suffered a great deal in agony and anguish, crying out, "My God, My God, why have you forsaken me?" And just the night before (in the Garden of Gethsemane), He prayed with a heartbreaking intensity that this cup of suffering be taken from Him. Still, He allowed the will of His Father to be done, ending His prayer with, "Not My will, but Yours."

It's not shocking that God's will for Jesus Christ was for Him to be accused falsely, tried in a kangaroo court, condemned without evidence, and brutally killed at the prime age of 33-½ years. If it were, we'd be in a mess today! God had a better plan, and out of the death of Jesus Christ came salvation for billions of souls.

When I grew older and more mature, the true meaning of Good Friday became evident. Jesus died a brutal death so that we should not die an eternal one; so that we would no longer be slaves to sin. What satan meant for bad, God used to redeem mankind and the cosmos, and He is now reconciling all those who call upon the name of Jesus.

It's likely that Jesus' disciples – on crucifixion day – wondered why, if He was so powerful, didn't He use those powers to free Himself? Some spectators had harsh words for him. Even one of the thieves crucified with Jesus Christ had his own words of mockery and disdain, challenging Him to save Himself.

> "'He saved others,' they said, 'but he can't save himself! He's the king of Israel! Let him come down now from the cross, and we will believe in him.'" (Matt. 27:42)

On the night Jesus Christ was betrayed and captured by authorities, His disciples ran away, deserting Him. These were the men Jesus had spent more than three years equipping and preparing to continue His ministry when He left earth. Even Peter, who had promised to die for Jesus Christ, denied Him three times while Jesus was watching.

Can you imagine how Jesus must have felt to be abandoned by those who were closest to Him? Still, all this suffering had a purpose, and Jesus did not waste it. He did not complain but embraced the cross willingly, and now He is sitting at the right hand of God the Father. Besides this highly elevated position, all authority in heaven, on earth, and under the earth has been given to Jesus Christ. At the mere mention of His name, all things in heaven, on earth and under the earth must bow and confess that He is Lord. Jesus endured the cross because of the reward set before Him. He understood that the momentary suffering He was going through was nothing compared to the glory that was to come.

We are to be imitators of Jesus Christ, for He is our example. We should not allow momentary setbacks to derail us from what we have been called to do. Many people complain that they can't do what they're called to do because they see the trials and tribulations in their lives as obstacles that need to be removed first. But the truth is that these obstacles are the very tools they need to move from where they are right now to where they want to be.

All Things Work Together for Good

We are still talking about what you already have. While most people always desire to have only good things happen to them and do all to avoid anything bad, they are missing out on how life works. No wonder many people are dissatisfied, perplexed, and depressed. Part of the reason is that they try to avoid pain, discomfort, and suffering at all costs. Therefore, when things do not go as they desire or plan, they easily feel crushed and frustrated.

There is a better and more effective way to look at life. What you have can be the good, the bad, or the ugly, and it can *still be useful*. In God's economy, everything is beneficial. Here is one of the most quoted Bible verses:

> "And we know that all things work together for good to those who love God, to those who are the called according to His purpose." (Rom. 8:28 NKJV)

When the Bible says ALL, it means ALL. You cannot cherry-pick what you think is more useful than the other. Many people only want the pay raise, yet still do all they can to avoid being fired. Until you are fired from your job, you may never be able to get a more comfortable and better-paying job. While the firing itself is painful, you should not lose sight of the great benefit that being let go brings.

You can only walk through one door; it's impossible to be at two places at the same time. When one door closes, another door will eventually open. The process of changing locations may be uncomfortable, but when you do, you may be surprised by what you encounter in the new place. Many people have been fired, justly or unjustly, only to realize that it was a *promotion in disguise*.

Therefore, instead of harboring anger, bitterness, and resentment towards those who unjustly fired you, it may be prudent for you to thank them.

Consider the example of Jesus Christ, who, after He had been betrayed, falsely accused, and crucified, asked God to forgive these people because they did not know what they were doing. In fact, they thought they were doing the work of God by killing the Messiah that everybody was waiting for.

The brothers of Joseph did not know that betraying him and selling him off as a slave to Egypt to die was actually helping to launch Joseph to become the leader he had dreamed of being. This is why Joseph could forgive his brothers when they finally reconnected. What Joseph's brothers did against him was so outrageous that their guilt followed them for a long time, even after Joseph forgave them.

Twenty years after their father, Jacob, had died, the brothers became afraid, going to Joseph and pleading for their lives. With their father now dead, they feared Joseph would punish them for what they had done against him. It is a pity these brothers lived their whole life in guilt because they allowed jealousy and envy to lead them.

But Joseph was not who they thought he was; listen to his response:

> "Joseph said to them, 'Do not be afraid, for am I in the place of God? But as for you, you meant evil against me; but God meant it for good, in order to bring it about as it is this day, to save many people alive. Now therefore, do not be afraid; I will provide for you and your little ones.' And he comforted them and spoke kindly to them." Genesis 50:19-21 (NKJV)

First, Joseph removed the attention from himself to God by acknowledging that he is not God. Then he also points out the evil his brothers did and the evil intention they had in their hearts. The paradox here is that while Joseph's brothers had an evil intention in their hearts, God had a good purpose in His heart. In the end, God's good purpose swallowed the evil.

There is a great lesson here that will save you a lot of anguish and headaches. You are not God, so do not try to second guess what would have happened if such-and-such had taken place – or not taken place.

Too many have been grounded, believing that events are responsible for outcomes. Champions don't think this way! We can't predict the future, and if Joseph had thought that way, he couldn't have used his condition as a slave and prisoner to prepare himself to become second-in-command in Egypt.

Rejoice Always

You are being asked to do the impossible because you lack what it takes to do it. When people ask, "Why me?" they end up discouraged, frustrated, and at times, some even take their own lives because they cannot bear under the circumstances. The simple reason is they have been conditioned to expect good things. Therefore, when bad things happen, they are ill-prepared and ill-equipped to handle them.

You will be able to rejoice always because now you know that God needs not only good things to perform miracles in your life, He can use *everything* that happens in your life. We are not in any way calling evil good. Evil is evil, it will never be good, but God's love and grace can always punctuate evil and make something good come of it.

Therefore, rejoice according to these comforting words from Paul the Apostle:

> "Rejoice always, pray without ceasing, in everything give thanks; for this is the will of God in Christ Jesus for you."
> (1 Thess. 5:16-18 NKJV)

Making the most of what you have even includes a job loss. Being single or unmarried is what you have. This means that every stage of your life is a good place for God to perform miracles.

The widow experienced multiplication because her husband died and left her penniless and indebted. If her husband had left her with a vast inheritance and no debt, she wouldn't have had any need that required Elisha's help.

Therefore, when you are facing obstacles, instead of asking, "Why me?" get excited, rejoice – you are about to get a promotion! A miracle is about to happen, and you will be the beneficiary of that miracle by virtue of where you are at the moment. Consider it a great joy that you have been counted worthy of going through that particular challenge and remember that there are testimonies to be had with each problem.

As I wrap up this issue of "Why me?" I must bring up something that happened in my life in 2010. I had been laid off in 2009 and could not get a job for a lack of work authorization. My current credentials were an H-1 B visa, conditioned on being employed by the company which had issued it. When I lost my job, I was – technically – out of status, in danger of deportation without finding another job via another H-1 B visa.

My only choice was to enroll in an MBA program; being in school meant I couldn't work. God had blessed us with four children, and at that time, my wife was jobless as well. Our situation was pitiful, to say the least, and some days I would weep from frustration and anger because I couldn't believe what we were going through.

Then, one day, a revelation put everything into perspective, allowing me to get through this stage of my life with grace and poise. The issue? No green card; it certainly wasn't a life or death issue, but it felt severe. Finally, able to embrace the situation as something that I had to go through for God to be glorified, I gained peace of mind and stopped complaining. I started anticipating what God would do and how the testimony would look.

Thanks be to God, not long after that, I got the news that brought tears to my eyes! While we'd been pushed up against the wall in terms of green cards, the decision to embrace the situation and let go of our worry made a big difference.

Ask the Diamond

The average person lets setbacks and adversities stop them, but champions have learned how to make use of the good, the bad, and the ugly.

There is a lot we can learn from natural processes because we are part of nature. When you look at some of the major breakthroughs and inventions, you will see that they mimic nature. For example, the design of the airplane mimics a bird. This is evident in the streamlined nature of the aircraft, the wings, and even the tail.

The internal combustion engine mimics what is happening in all animals, including us. The food we eat has the sun's energy that has been trapped in it. When we eat the food and breathe in oxygen, it oxidizes the food, and energy is released that powers our bodies. The oxidation of the hydrocarbons in our bodies produces by-products such as water and CO_2.

This is the same process that is taking place in the internal combustion engine – complex hydrocarbons are in the form of gasoline, and then internal combustion in the engine is created by the introduction of oxygen. Energy is released from this process, powering the automobile to move from one place to another. The by-products are water and CO_2.

Jesus himself used many different natural processes to convey spiritual truths because He recognized that the natural could be a great source of inspiration. We can reproduce what is naturally happening because we know it will work.

Let me introduce you to one of the wonders of nature and let it teach you what you can do with pressure and stressful and uncomfortable situations in which you find yourself.

Diamonds are forever and have fascinated mankind for a long time. From the blood diamonds of Liberia to the Kohinoor diamond, which is part of the British Crown Jewels, diamonds command much respect. There is no substance harder than diamond. Because of this exceptional hardness, diamonds have many industrial uses and are so resistant to erosion/abrasion that DeBeers coined the term "A Diamond is Forever."

How do diamonds form, and what makes them so valuable? For a diamond to form, it needs extremely high temperatures of about 2000 °F. These conditions are found in the uppermost part of the mantle at a depth of about 90 miles below the surface of the earth. The pressure at this depth is about 725,000 pounds per square inch. This is an immense amount of pressure.

When you combine this high temperature with pressure and introduce carbon, diamonds are formed. Instead of complaining about the excessively high temperatures and pressure, the carbon arranges itself in a tightly packed tetrahedral structure.

The dense structure of diamond, making it an extremely hard material, owes itself to the extremely high temperatures and pressures under which it is formed. Diamonds hold a unique place in our lives because, from inception, it was uniquely fashioned for a particular purpose. If the diamond could complain, though, it would cry out for cooler temperatures and less pressure!

Nobody wants to be under heat and pressure, but through this heat and pressure, giants are made.

When you compare the diamond to granite, you will understand what I mean. Graphite is made up of carbon, but the conditions under which it is formed differ from those of diamonds. While diamond forms deep in the earth under high temperature and pressure, graphite forms near the surface of the earth under low temperature and pressure. No wonder graphite is soft and used in pencils.

Graphite can be used in making things like pencils, but a diamond cannot; it is too hard. Conversely, diamonds are highly-priced and used for more noble purposes, especially gem-quality diamonds. In other words, the diamond and graphite were fashioned under different circumstances for different purposes. One cannot replace the other because they are uniquely different and have different purposes.

Do you know what your purpose is? Have you been called to be a diamond or graphite? Do you know that the current pressure and fires you are in right now may just be fashioning you to become what you are being called to be? Don't waste the trials, troubles, and tribulations in your life – they may be your passport to the life you have always wanted to live!

While you may not have the opportunity to choose what pressures and difficulties come into your life, you have the privilege of choosing how you respond. You can respond in hope, optimism, and a positive attitude, focusing on the fact that you are fortunate to be under this preparation process for the assignment ahead of you. Or you may become negative, donning a complaining and regretful attitude because you want to be someone else and in a different place.

Before you pray to escape your circumstances, remember: you may be on your way to becoming a diamond!

Nobody says this better than James the Apostle:

> "My brethren, count it all joy when you fall into various trials, knowing that the testing of your faith produces patience. But let patience have its perfect work, that you may be perfect and complete, lacking nothing." (James 1:2-4 NKJV)

This is why you should get excited when things are heating up around you; because you know that you will lack nothing when you go through the difficulties. The two widows who used what they already had moved into abundance and lack became a thing of the past in their lives.

As much as the question "Why me?" is appealing, it leads to a dead end. Instead, ask, "Why not me?" Then, you are embracing the situation, and taking responsibility, choosing to become a victor – not a victim. This is a winning attitude that will give you the courage and strength to go through anything that comes your way.

In the next chapter, we'll be talking about how to put what you have learned into practice because, without action, you will not be able to achieve anything. But you must be willing to take that essential first step.

CHAPTER 6

Babies Start Small
for a Reason

The message in this book is centered around identifying what you already have and making use of it; however, without an adequate understanding of what you already have, you cannot make use of it. We have already seen different circumstances where great miracles happened because people used what they had on hand.

Many people do not make use of what they already have because it requires them to take responsibility for their circumstances, and many don't want to work hard for anything. You can't reap without sowing! Others simply don't want to wait for results; we live in a microwave generation accustomed to instant gratification. When you tell people to wait, you lose them.

People Do Not Want to Start Small

Starting small is antithetical to most people. The thought of starting as a nobody and slowly working their way to the top makes them want to give up before they start. This explains why many people are looking to get-rich-quick schemes. Others are looking for quick fixes, even if it means neglecting the root causes of the problem.

We do not need to look far to realize that such thinking and expectations are faulty; nature doesn't teach this! Babies start small for a reason, and a mother can't carry an adult in her womb.

In his book "The 7 Habits of Highly Effective People," Stephen Covey writes, "In all life, there are sequential stages of growth and development. A child learns to turn, to sit up, to crawl, and then to walk and run. Each step is important, and each one takes time. No step can be skipped."

The message in this book is positive, so let's not get bogged down with the reasons we are not making use of what we already have. Instead, let's focus on how we can make use of what we already have.

You may be wondering how making use of what you already have works in the real world. There is no "one size fits all" – each person's situation is different and unique – but there are universal principles that can be applied across the board.

Below are some principles to incorporate into your life; you'll need this practical hands-on approach in discovering what you already have and how to use it.

You Must Start Small

The choice to start small is not oppositional; it is compulsory because it is built in your DNA. All of us began as tiny cells. In fact, about twenty of us could fit on the tip of a needle! Through the process of repeated cell divisions, we grew with each passing day, eventually reaching the point where we could survive outside of the womb. We were born, and the cell division process continued until we became adults.

When you start small, you build the capacity you need to handle the increases ahead. This is why if you take on more than you can manage, you suffer burnout; your productivity – and eventually your health – suffers. Jesus Christ taught about the benefits of starting small:

> "He who is faithful in what is least is faithful also in much, and he who is unjust in what is least is unjust also in much. Therefore, if you have not been faithful in the unrighteous mammon, who will commit to your trust the true riches?"
> (Luke 16:10-11 NKJV)

You will become what you consistently do. Unfortunately, many people think that they can build bad habits and change them as soon as the opportunity presents itself. This is the highest form of self-deception because when the time comes, they will not change.

If it were that easy to change our habits, we would all be healthy, wealthy, and famous. There would be no need for a book like this one, because everybody would not only know what they should be doing, they would *actually do it*.

Not too long ago, I heard a confession from someone about their failure to exercise. This individual knows that exercising regularly is good – they even hired a personal trainer and paid for a gym membership.

In the gym parking lot one day, his phone rang, and his personal trainer relayed that he'd be unable to train that day. He turned his car around and drove back home, taking the absence of his trainer as an excuse to do nothing. The habit of not exercising was stronger than that of exercising.

Contrast this with those who exercise consistently and persistently no matter what the weather is. They exercise in the summer, winter, spring, and fall. Nothing seems to stop them from exercising. These individuals do not necessarily enjoy exercising, but they do it anyway. There are days when everything in their bodies tells them not to go out and exercise, but they persist. Bad weather doesn't stop them because they have built such a strong habit that it delivers each time the need arises.

It takes more than a day to get to this type of dedication. I am writing from experience because my wife and I have been exercising five days a week consistently for almost a decade now.

When we started, we would miss some days because early in the morning, especially in winter, it was more comfortable to be under the warm blankets than go out in the cold. We would get up and ask each other if we should go out or not. When that question was posed, we would check our feelings, and 99.9 percent of the time, if the morning were too cold, our feelings would vote for us not to go out; we sheepishly obeyed.

One slight adjustment made a huge and lasting impact on us. We decided to stop asking whether we should go out and exercise when we got up in the morning. We just decided that when we got up, we would go out and exercise no matter what happened. Then we followed through, and with time, we have built such a strong habit that the first thing that comes to our minds when we get up in the morning is to go out and exercise.

This does not mean we don't struggle to exercise or that it is the most pleasurable thing to do in the morning. We enjoy it sometimes, but most days we endure it because of the benefits of exercising.

You must show commitment, in the least. For example, can you commit to walking a mile a day? When you do this over some time, you can increase it to two miles, then three miles. From walking, you can start running. Again, you will not start by running ten miles but will begin with a little, and slowly build it up.

It has become a regular practice of mine to run a marathon at the end of each month, but I did not start by running marathons. Over the years, I have slowly built the resistance and tenacity to run a marathon, and now it is paying off.

While you may be saying this exercise thing is not for you, don't forget that you can apply this principle to other areas of your life. This implies that before you ask for more, you must take care of the least. While it is comforting to think that a day will come when you have all the resources you need to launch a business venture, you should start making use of the little you already have.

Before You Manage a Million-Dollar Business

Some people want to start a multi-million dollar business without having managed a one-hundred-thousand dollar business. This is the same as saying that a child will move from crawling to running in the Olympics overnight. As outrageous as this illustration may sound, it highlights the foolishness of trying to circumvent the process. The sad thing is that such people do nothing but wait for things to happen for them. When asked why they don't start, their response is usually centered on a lack of resources.

But the little they *do have* is often discounted and discarded. With each passing year, they get more and more frustrated and disillusioned because they have refused to use what they have.

How many people die with excellent ideas that would have made a significant difference in the world because they refused to make use of the little they already had?

Do you want real treasures? Then you must learn how to be faithful with the little that you already have. Complaining and giving excuses and feeling that other people have more than you are a dead end. The miracle you are expecting is already in your hands. All you need to do is show some degree of commitment and dedication, and the increase will come.

You Must Take Care of Other People's Things

Nothing is more revealing about a person's character than taking care of what is not theirs. The story of Cinderella, and many other such tales, fascinate us because we can quickly identify with the underdogs in these stories.

We all know that Cinderella was not the daughter of the woman who was raising her; her stepmother showed preferential treatment to her own daughters, ensuring they had the best of everything. At the same time, she mistreated Cinderella, but when the opportunity came for her daughters to marry the prince, they failed miserably. Cinderella, the neglected, insulted, and abused one, got what this woman desired strongly for her own daughters.

Things worked out for Cinderella because, even though this woman mistreated her, she continued to work hard and take care of the woman and her daughters. There is no indication that she became lazy, careless, or slothful. Instead, she continued cooking, cleaning, and mending dresses. While she was working hard, the woman's real daughters were having fun.

Are you known for being faithful to other people's property? How do you treat the property of the company you are working for? Do you show up to work and do just the bare minimum, or do you handle the job like your own and give it your all? Are you always looking for ways to take out more than you put in? While the company may not be doing their part, are you faithfully doing yours?

These days, loyalty has been thrown out of the window because many people only ask, "What's in it for me?" How can you put in the least amount of effort and reap a huge reward?

When this type of limited thinking is challenged, some people justify it by saying that they are just doing what the company is doing to them. In other words, because the company is unfair to them, they will pay back the company in the same way.

I call this "limited thinking" because individuals who behave like this don't believe that they may own and run a company one day. If they knew that they'd be running a company and needing help from other people, they might reconsider their behavior while employed by others.

Therefore, if you want to excel in the future, you have to excel where you are *right now*. If the company is not treating you well, you should look for a better place instead of staying where you are but not doing what you are being paid to do.

The subject of working under unfavorable conditions brings back the story of Joseph. He had been sold in Egypt into slavery by his brothers, who wanted him dead. While in Egypt, Joseph was sold a second time to Potiphar. In Potiphar's house Joseph, even though a slave, worked diligently and excellently. His hard work paid off as his master's businesses prospered. Joseph was so good at what he was doing that he was put in charge of all his master's affairs.

Then Joseph refused to commit adultery and was thrown in jail. This was totally unfair because his master's wife lied about the whole thing, yet Joseph was faithful in prison, and his hard work gained him a promotion.

While Joseph was physically enslaved, he was internally free because he kept working hard and being productive. The leadership skills and administrative skills he was honing would someday come to his rescue, bringing him freedom and making him second-in-command in Egypt.

Joseph could have thrown a pity party and refused to serve his masters, but he understood that taking care of other people's things was preparing him to take care of his own eventually. This may sound counter-intuitive, but consider the following admonition from Jesus Christ:

> "And if you have not been faithful in what is another man's, who will give you what is your own?" (Luke 16:12 NKJV)

Jesus asked a very pointed question that everyone needs to consider. Have you been faithful in what you already have, even though it may not be yours? If the answer is yes, then you should be excited because your reward is on the way. You will have your own soon.

Note that the question is not, "Have you been treated well by the person whose things you are taking care of?" While fairness should be practiced by all, you mustn't forget that you are the person to set the pace. If you allow the failures of other people (or their actions/inactions) to determine the outcome of your life, you have yourself to blame.

You are not at the mercy of what happens to you but can choose the right response. Focus on developing yourself, allowing others to be themselves; you account for no one but yourself.

In this chapter, we emphasized the importance of starting small and even starting by taking care of someone else's things first. In the next chapter, we will focus on all we have discussed so far, seeing how it fits into a life of unlimited abundance. You have made it this far, and I am so proud of your commitment and dedication. Let's finish strong!

CHAPTER SEVEN

Unlimited Productivity

If you are like many people, you desire to be successful and experience abundance in every aspect of your life. It is a good thing to have the ambition to be at the top and to do well. The desire for success and increase is built into us. After nine months in our mother's womb, we figured out that the womb was too small, and it was time to make the grand exit. We knew it was time to move out into the world and start using our hands, feet, fingers, and all the different body parts we had grown.

Why is it that after we are born, at a certain point, we stop asking questions, taking risks, and become afraid to make mistakes and fail? Most people stop being children and start being adults. What this means is that they start caring more about what others think about them than what they think of themselves, and the desire to fit in becomes stronger than the desire to stand up for what they believe.

In this chapter, we will be focusing on how to tap into the unlimited potential within you and unleash unrestricted growth in every area of your life.

Before we get into the details of how to do this, let's take a moment and see what the Master Jesus Christ Himself did. There is much to learn from this incident where Jesus Christ feeds 5,000 people with two fish and five loaves of bread. This was not an easy thing to do, but we will see that, with God, all things are possible.

Meet Jesus Christ

To this point, we have focused on instances that took place in the Old Testament; let's move over into the New Testament to show the principle of using what you have, providing us with even more reasons to make sure we're living our lives in accordance with this powerful principle.

The feeding of the five thousand solidifies this principle because, as we are about to see, Jesus Christ did more than just feed the hungry crowd – and He is ready to do more in your life as well. Jesus fed a large crowd twice, but we will focus on the time He fed 5,000 (including women and children) because both miracles have many similarities.

Before this great miracle, we are told that Jesus had just heard about the death of John the Baptist, His cousin. That is John, who had announced the coming of the Lamb of God who would increase while John decreased. In fact, it is John who baptized Jesus and boldly declared to the people that Jesus was the Lamb of God, He who takes away the sins of the world. John had preached against King Herod for taking his brother's wife – a message that didn't sit well with Herod's wife, who then instigated John's imprisonment; finally, he was decapitated because of her.

A challenging concept: why didn't Jesus free John when he was in prison? John had sent some of his disciples to ask Jesus Christ if indeed He was the Messiah. Jesus did not follow through to get John out of prison and allowed him to be beheaded. When this happened, John's disciples came and told Jesus that His cousin had been brutally and gruesomely killed.

We are told that when Jesus heard this sad news, He withdrew to a solitary place. I cannot imagine what Jesus was thinking at that time, but it must have reminded Him that His own time to die a brutal death was not too far away. In God's economy, nothing is wasted. This is why you must understand that insomuch as you desire to see God bring an increase in your life, He – and He alone – has the final say. You must submit your will to God and trust Him with the outcome.

Back to our story! While Jesus Christ was trying to catch His breath and process what was happening, a large crowd discovered where He was and showed up. Instead of getting angry and sending the crowd away, it is written:

> "When Jesus landed and saw a large crowd,
> he had compassion on them and healed their
> sick." (Matt. 14:14)

Jesus was moved by compassion, even though He was
dealing with the loss of His cousin; this demonstrates
His heart of love. This is something that we have to learn
– how to show compassion toward other people. When
we begin to walk in compassion, we will experience
supernatural multiplication and miracles in our lives as
well. In other words, we will have the fortitude and
tenacity to go the extra mile and do that we usually
would not be able to. When we have compassion, we
can tap into the ability to do the impossible – and
provide solutions beyond our greatest imagination.

Identifying the Problem is Not Enough

We live in a world that has too many problems. Billions
of people live in abject poverty without access to
clean water, proper nutrition, education, safety, etc.
This is common information because we see the
World Vision commercials on TV and read about war,
famine, corruption, and poor governance taking place
all over the world. But this is just the first step towards
a solution. It is not enough to *know* what is happening.
We can easily blame these people for causing their
predicament, or we can have compassion and do
something.

Unfortunately, many people ease their consciences and
justify their reason for not doing something because
they think the problem is too huge, and there is nothing

they can do. Many become overwhelmed and do what the disciples did:

> "As evening approached, the disciples came to him and said, 'This is a remote place, and it's already getting late. Send the crowds away, so they can go to the villages and buy themselves some food.'"(Matt. 14:15)

This was a large crowd in a remote area, and the disciples knew a problem was brewing: dinnertime was coming, people would be hungry, and something had to be done – and done fast. We must commend the disciples of Jesus for identifying the problem, but their solution was not suitable.

According to them, sending the people away would ensure that they did not have to deal with the problem themselves. The people were the ones who were going to become hungry, and it was on them to look for something to eat. This way of thinking made sense. After all, Jesus had spoken to them freely, not even passing an offering basket to collect money. Must the people be fed as well?

Have you identified problems that need fixing? It can be in your life, community, country, or the world. Do you feel too insignificant to come up with a solution? You do not have to feel overwhelmed. The problem was shown to you – or you have been able to see the problem – because you already have a solution.

While driving our girls to school, I heard what Mother Theresa told some nuns who came to work with her in Calcutta. She told them, "There are many 'Calcuttas' in the world, go and find yours and take care of it." This was not some sort of a rebuke to those trying to work with her, but encouragement for them to find their voice and sing their own song.

Not all of us have the same assignment, and we should not be afraid to pursue that which we have been called to do. There are so many opportunities to make a difference in our world; none of us should feel we do not have something meaningful to do. What we need the most is compassion and love for others; *that* will propel us toward doing the impossible.

Do the Impossible

I am glad that the disciples went to Jesus after they came up with their action plan. Had they implemented it without asking Jesus, it would have been a disaster; they would have missed seeing the miracle that Jesus performed, and missed having a firsthand experience of what compassion and love for other people can do.

When they presented their plan to Jesus, He asked them to do the impossible:

> "Jesus replied, 'They do not need to go away. You give them something to eat.'" (Matt. 14:16)

Can you imagine how terrified and perplexed the disciples must have been? Jesus was telling them to do the impossible by asking them to feed all these thousands of people. How in the world could they feed this many people when there was no place around to buy the food, even if they had the money? This was inconceivable!

Why didn't Jesus just go ahead and provide the food that the people needed? After all, He is God and could have easily commanded bread and meat to come down from heaven for the people to eat. But, He didn't. He wanted the disciples to participate in this miracle. Second, Jesus wanted to teach them the importance of making use of what they already had. Third, letting go of what you have for others will always bring increase and multiplication.

Do you feel that you are being called to do the impossible, or that you are facing a hopeless situation? You are not alone and should not dismay; the disciples had no clue what to do when asked to do the impossible.

It Is Possible

The reaction of the disciples was typical because they focused on how big their challenge was. When you focus solely on whatever challenge you may be facing, the next reaction will be to start complaining. The sole purpose of this book is to help you stop complaining.

The disciples complained to Jesus about their lack of resources to feed the thousands of people that were gathered:

"'We have here only five loaves of bread and
two fish,' they answered. 'Bring them here to
me,' He said. And He directed the people to
sit down on the grass. Taking the five loaves
and the two fish and looking up to heaven, He
gave thanks and broke the loaves. Then He
gave them to the disciples, and the disciples
gave them to the people. They all ate and were
satisfied, and the disciples picked up twelve
basketfuls of broken pieces that were left over.
The number of those who ate was about five
thousand men, besides women and children."
(Matt. 14:17-21)

Complaining is a widespread reaction, generally used
to solicit sympathy from others and make excuses for
not taking necessary action. It is incredible that the
disciples quickly found the five loaves of bread and
two fish. Did they bring them to Jesus to show Him
how dire the situation was? Did they have any idea that
Jesus was going to multiply it?

While we don't know the answers to those questions,
we do know that they brought the little that they already
had and presented it to Jesus. Then Jesus instructed
them what to do. Again, as in the case of Moses and
the two widows, the disciples and the people had to do
something ridiculous that did not make any sense at
all. Can you imagine the disciples taking the bread and
the fish from Jesus and wondering what would happen
next? They had been instructed to ask the people to
sit down, and some of the people might have asked

why. The disciples may have been fearful, whispering to them that dinner was about to be served. "But where is the food going to come from?" some might have asked. "Well, just wait and see," they may have responded. The people and the disciples had to obey the instructions for the miracle to happen.

It must have been shocking and perplexing when the first person took the bread, broke it, and gave it to another person and another person and another person – and the bread was not diminishing, but instead increasing and increasing. This is not what they were expecting to see because it was out of the norm. They had never witnessed anything of this magnitude.

It Is About Others

It's not about you, but about what you can do for others. Do not worry that if you focus on taking care of other people, your own needs will not be met.

All the miracles of multiplication we have seen had something to do with other people. When the disciples saw that the crowd was hungry, they wanted to do something for them. They took the initiative and reported the situation to Jesus, who was moved with compassion for the people and provided a solution that led to abundance. The five loaves of bread and two fish were multiplied and fed 5,000 men, not counting women and children, and twelve baskets of remaining food were collected.

Do not buy into the popular message of taking care only of yourself. When you position yourself to be blessed, do not forget that you are blessed in order to be a blessing. If you want to be a conduit of great benefits, develop compassion for others.

In every society in our world, there are many problems that need solutions. It does not matter where you live; if you look closely, you will see needs that must be met. This is an opportunity for you to experience the miracle of multiplication. Be willing to help other people and make your life available to make a difference for others.

Start small, follow instructions, and see how your life will flourish and become a blessing – not just to you, but to countless others.

Learn to Give

Are you aware of the needs of other people, or do you consider only your own needs? Having a heart of generosity does not come naturally for many people. Jesus made the following promise about giving:

> "Give, and it will be given to you: good measure, pressed down, shaken together, and running over will be put into your bosom. For with the same measure that you use, it will be measured back to you." (Luke 6:38 NKJV)

To have a life of unlimited productivity, you must make giving part of your life. The promise that Jesus gave was to encourage us to be generous, but for many, that's a struggle because they worry they are losing something when they give. This is not true, because it is more blessed to give than to receive.

When you give, you initiate the *receiving process*. To give, your hand is open, and you are creating the room to receive because something is leaving you. In other words, it is advantageous for you to give.

We can learn much from plants. Most produce a lot of seeds from just one single seed. They usually contain the tree and all the other seeds that tree will produce. All this great potential and increase is locked in the seed, no matter how large or small the seed is.

But for the seed to become a tree that will eventually produce many seeds, it must die. When a seed is planted, it gives up being a seed to become a tree. What the seed gives away is its form, color, and all the external things that made it a seed. In this process of losing itself, the seed is actually remaking itself, and it will make great gains through this loss. What the seed gains is thousands of times more than the single seed that it gives away.

View giving from this perspective: There is a profound, spiritual, underlying principle that underpins giving. If you do not give, you will not receive.

Do you know why lakes, rivers and even the ocean evaporate? Because they need to receive something. When the water evaporates, it will finally condense and fall back in the form of rain that eventually finds its way back to the ocean.

Through this process, the water creates a lot of good before returning to the lake or ocean. You can see that since the lakes, rivers, and oceans refuse to be selfish and permanently hold the water, every drop is used repeatedly for a long time. Can you imagine what would happen if the water from the rivers, lakes, and ocean was held permanently? There would be no water to share with the rest of the earth; our planet would not be what it is today.

While most people only think about money when giving is mentioned, money is not the only thing that can be given. There are many other things you can give and, through them, experience multiplication and unlimited productivity.

Jesus took five loaves of bread and two fish, blessed them, and gave them to the apostles to give to the people. When the apostles obeyed and gave to the people, they experienced a supernatural increase and super-abundant productivity.

Before you say that you have nothing to give, remember that money is not the only thing that can be given. The greatest resource that we all have an equal amount of is time. You can give your time to help other people. You can use your story to inspire and give encouragement.

Remember how the widow was instructed to use her last flour and oil to make a cake? Then she had to give it to the prophet Elijah to eat, even though she and her son would have nothing left to eat. Yet, when she followed the instructions and gave, she experienced supernatural productivity. Her flour and oil ran freely until the drought ended.

When you are a giver, your own economy will differ from the general economy because you are operating by a supernatural principle.

Take the case of the widow. It did not matter that there was a drought in the land, and things were difficult. When she obeyed the instructions given to her by Elijah, she stepped into an entirely different economy. While others were living in lack, she had more than enough.

You, too, can live a life of abundance when you begin to give. Don't worry that when you uplift and empower other people, they will have more than you; instead, develop an abundance mindset – that of a giver – and you will never suffer lack again.

Have Compassion

Are you a compassionate person? Do you feel for others? When you see other people suffering, are you moved to do something to help alleviate their suffering? To have compassion for people demands that you go beyond just feeling sorry for them. You must *do something* for those whom you think need help.

The miracle of feeding five-thousand people with so little food was driven by compassion. Jesus Christ had compassion on the masses because they were hungry and tired. There are many hungry and tired people in the world, and you can do something for them if you have enough compassion.

The Path to Compassion

It may seem that you are being asked to do something beyond your ability. This call to compassion, living a life of unlimited productivity and impact, may appear to be beyond your capability.

If this is how you are feeling right now, don't panic! I want you to meet Jesus Christ, the only person who can work this miracle through you. There is nothing more important than being connected to God. While many may argue that there is one God and many different roads to this God, I will object to that conclusion; because all the religions in the world have different gods, there is no need for all the gods to be the same.

Some are incredibly uncomfortable to hold any discussion that involves God because they do not want to offend people. The problem with such a world view is that such people are treating something casually that is extremely important. We all know that if we have a diagnosis of brain cancer, we will not want just any doctor to operate on our brain. Anybody who is wise will look for the "best of the best" to conduct the surgery.

You will meticulously gather knowledge about the different specialists available and gain some understanding of what separates them. Then you will make an informed and wise decision, selecting the best to operate on your brain. You do not hold a vote and decide what doctor will operate on your brain based on popular support or which doctor is trending, as long as the doctor is competent and has the necessary skills and expertise to take care of you.

Then why is it that, when it comes to spiritual matters, people seem not to be as diligent as they ought to be? Is it because they do not know what is at stake? May I suggest that your soul is more important than your physical body? In fact, there is no price tag for your soul. All the wealth in the world is not enough to buy your soul. Therefore, pay close attention to your soul's eternal destiny.

I am not trying to force you to embrace some particular religious tradition; I am not a religious person. What I am suggesting here is that you carefully consider the claims that Jesus Christ made and what He has accomplished for you already. My sincere hope is that you will put in the time and effort necessary to acquire the right knowledge and gain the understanding that you need to make a wise decision regarding the eternal destiny of your soul.

There is nothing more important than your soul. And you do not need the approval of others to make things right with God. On the contrary, making things right with God is an individual decision, and it is not popular. Consider the following statement that Jesus Christ made:

> "Enter by the narrow gate; for wide is the gate and broad is the way that leads to destruction, and there are many who go in by it. Because narrow is the gate and difficult is the way which leads to life, and there are few who find it." (Matt. 7:13-14 NKJV)

According to this verse, there are too many people who are walking on the road to destruction. This implies that if you only follow what's popular, you will end up in destruction. There is no need to follow the crowd. Get on the narrow path that few are walking, and you will find life. This is not just any type of life; it is eternal life that Jesus Christ Himself gives. Here is your opportunity to get on the path of eternal life. Don't allow what is popular and trending to rob you of eternal life!

I want to say, "Congratulations!" You have done what many people do not. Most people start books and never finish reading them. Yet you persevered, and now you are here.

There is nothing more important than being a child of God. I would be wicked if I did not share this truth with you. It is one of the most important things you will ever do. It is more important than taking care of your physical body because your body will eventually decay.

Acknowledgment

My first thanks go to my Heavenly Father, the source of all things, including wisdom, knowledge, and inspiration. The message in this book was an inspiration of the Holy Spirit more than twenty years ago, and over the years, God has faithfully demonstrated the power of this message in my own life. I am grateful and appreciative of the privilege of being a bearer of this message and for the strength and tenacity that God has given to me to put this together.

Many people have contributed to shaping my understanding of making use of what we have, experiencing great multiplication because of it. I want to give a special thank you to my parents for their input, and for demonstrating how to achieve much with little.

A special thank you to my wife for being adventurous enough in agreeing to start life with me, with very little to show for it. She made it possible for us to live, and still live, the message presented in this book. I am a stronger believer in making use of what we have because she agreed to marry me when I proposed to her, even though I was a poor student who had little to show.

A big thank you to our children, Afaamboma, Ntsongmboma, Elotmboma, Abeutmboma, and Atesamboma for their support and encouragement. Above all, they have, time and again, demonstrated the power of making the most of what we already have by not allowing anything to stop them from expressing their love and appreciation for me.

Writing a book is not something that one does alone. We get information and support from other people directly, standing on the shoulders of many people to see what lies ahead. What I have written in this book did not originate from me. I have quoted Moses, Elijah, Elisha, and the two widows whose obedience laid the foundation for the message in this book.

Without the dedication of the editorial team, who transformed the manuscript into something that can be read, this book would not have seen the light of day. I do not know what I would do without the editorial team. A big thank you for all the hard work and significant input.

The design team also did a fantastic job of laying out the book, and I am incredibly grateful for their dedication and commitment to this project.

A special thank you to all my readers who keep encouraging me to write more and for your feedback. You are the reason I keep writing.

Author's Biography

D r. Eric Tangumonkem was born and raised in a caldera on the Cameroon Volcanic Line in Cameroon, West Africa. He has a Bachelor's Degree in Geology and a minor in Sociology from the University of Buea in Cameroon, a Masters in Earth Sciences from the University of Yaounde in Cameroon, and a Doctorate in Geosciences from the University of Texas at Dallas. In addition to being a geoscientist with extensive experience in the oil and gas industry, he is a teacher and an entrepreneur.

Currently, he teaches at Embry Riddle Aeronautical University, and West Hills College. He is also the President of IEM Approach, a premier personal growth and leadership development company based on the infinite wisdom revealed over the ages. He is on a mission to inspire, equip, and motivate people from all walks of life to find their God-given purpose, and to pursue and possess it. He is married and has five children.

Available for speaking engagements:

If you want to invite Dr. Tangumonkem to come and speak, you can call him using this number 214-908-3963 or email him at eternalkingdom101@gmail.com

Here are his social media handles:

https://www.erictangumonkem.com

https://www.linkedin.com/in/drtangumonkem/

https://twitter.com/DrTangumonkem

https://www.facebook.com/drtangumonkem

tangumonkem.tumblr.com

https://instagram.com/tangumonkem/

http://www.pinterest.com/erictangumonkem/

https://vimeo.com/user23079930

https://www.youtube.com/c/EricTangumonkem

Other Resources
by the Author

Coming to America: A Journey of Faith

Do you struggle with trusting God with your finances? Feel that God is calling you to do something big but you can't see how it will be accomplished? Fear that He has abandoned you after starting your journey of faith? Coming to America: A Journey of Faith is Eric Tangumonkem's story of wrestling with these thoughts and doubts. God called him to America from Cameroon to pursue graduate studies at the University of Texas at Dallas, but he had no money to put towards this dream. In this book, Tangumonkem shares his journey of learning to trust God as he stepped out in faith and came to America despite a lack of funds. He also shares some of his formative experiences prior to this call-experiences that will encourage readers in their faith. Tangumonkem's life is a testimony to the faithfulness of God, and he is careful to give Him all of the glory.

https://www.amazon.com/dp/B082D16PD5/ref=cm_sw_r_tw_dp_x_RXTmFbKTVRZCR via @amazon

The Use and Abuse of Titles in The Church

This book examines reasons behind the disturbing proliferation of titles in Christendom in recent times by seven distinguished Christian professionals. The book challenges readers to stay on the straight and narrow road, which celebrates ministers with titles bestowed based on sound Biblical foundations, while shunning those with titles associated with self-promotion and doctrinal errors. The book also provides the following actionable insights:· How to identify the proper use of titles · A history on the use of titles in Christendom How to avoid the pitfalls of acquiring bogus titles An understanding of the relationship between titles and leadership

https://www.amazon.com/dp/B01E5H36CC/ref=cm_sw_r_tw_dp_x_b4TmFb2K22RPE via @amazon

Seven Success Keys Learned From My Father

This is a book about my father, my teacher, my role model and hero. A man of passion like any other man, but a man of exceptional qualities and abilities as well. The following are the seven keys to success my father passed to me: Fear of God, Humility, Education, Integrity, Hard work, Prayer and Vision. All these keys have been instrumental in making me who I am today. In addition to these keys, my father was present when we were growing up. He made it a point of duty to talk the talk and walk the walk before us. This book illustrates how these seven keys to success were interwoven in our day-to-day lives and how they have opened unprecedented doors of success to me. My sincere prayer for you as you read this book is that these keys will open all doors for you and bring the success you desire so strongly. Amen!

https://www.amazon.com/dp/B01N0A0YYC/ref=cm_sw_r_tw_dp_x_I6TmFbP3QSX91 via @amazon

Viajando a América: Un Camino de Fe (Spanish Edition)

¿Lucha con confiar en Dios con sus finanzas? Siente que Dios le está llamando a hacer algo grande, pero usted no puede ver la forma en que se llevará a cabo? ¿Teme a que Él le ha abandonado después de comenzar su camino de fe?

Viajando a América: Un Camino de Fe es la historia de Eric Tangumonkem, de su lucha con estos pensamientos y dudas. Dios lo llamó a América desde Camerún para realizar estudios de posgrado en la Universidad de Texas en Dallas, pero no tenía dinero para seguir este llamado. En este libro, Tangumonkem comparte su viaje de aprender a confiar en Dios cuando caminó en la fe y llegó a Estados Unidos a pesar de su falta de fondos. También comparte algunas de sus experiencias formativas previas a esta convocatoria-experiencias que estimularán a los lectores en su fe. La vida de Tangumonkem es un testimonio de la fidelidad de Dios, y él tiene cuidado en darle toda la.

https://www.amazon.com/dp/B018H9S2BY/ref=cm_sw_r_tw_dp_x_hdUmFb8QN2148 via @amazon

MON ODYSSÉS AMÉRICAINE: UNE EXPÉRIENCE DE FOI (French Edition)

As-tu du mal à confier tes soucis financiers au Seigneur? Ressens-tu que Dieu t'appelle à faire quelque chose de grand, mais tu ne sais comment cela va se réaliser? Crains-tu qu'il va t'abandonner en chemin? Mon Odyssée Américaine: une expérience de foi est l'histoire d'Éric Tangumonkem et de sa lutte contre le doute et les pensées susmentionnées. Dieu l'a appelé depuis le Cameroun pour aller poursuivre ses études supérieures à l'Université du Texas à Dallas, mais il n'avait pas d'argent pour réaliser ce rêve. Dans ce livre, le Dr Tangumonkem partage avec vous les péripéties de son voyage qui l'ont amené à faire davantage confiance à Dieu alors qu'il se rendit aux États-Unis par la foi. Il partage également certaines des expériences qui l'ont bâti avant même son appel – expériences qui vont encourager les lecteurs dans leur foi. La vie du Dr Tangumonkem est un témoignage de la fidélité de Dieu à qui il rend toute la gloire.

https://www.amazon.com/dp/B00T7XBPMS/ref=cm_sw_r_tw_dp_x_heUmFbZH8NZWN via @amazon

God's Supernatural Agenda: 7 Secrets to Lasting Wealth and Prosperity

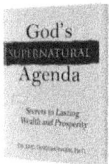

Is there something more valuable than money, precious stones, silver, and gold? Do you desire to be wealthy and prosperous? Are you already wealthy and prosperous, yet you feel empty and unsatisfied? Are you uncomfortable talking about money because it is "the root of all evil"? This book will not present shortcuts or get-rich-quick schemes, but important principles, laws, and processes involved in generating lasting wealth. You see, God desires for ALL of us to prosper today and for all eternity. He has a divine reason for that desire, and He has given us the way to attain it. God's Supernatural Agenda: 7 Secrets to Lasting Wealth and Prosperity presents His blueprint for prosperity and explains why it is what truly matters.

https://www.amazon.com/dp/B07WJLB4BM/ref=cm_sw_r_tw_dp_x_QfUmFb11KQQN0 via @amazon

Racism, Where Is Your Sting?
A provocative look at the beginning and the end of racism

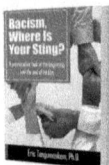

Each time the issue of racism is mentioned, tensions immediately run high, reason is thrown out the window, and emotional outbursts run rampant. Even though a lot of effort has been done to fight it, the devastating consequences continue to this day.

In this book, Dr. Tangumonkem challenges the status quo and presents a perspective that is both provocative and inspirational. Contrary to what you hear from those stoking the flames of racism and fermenting hate and bigotry, we are not at the mercy of racism. In fact, he dives deep into history to explain why the tendency to be racist is present in each one of us, regardless of skin color. The good news is that the victory has already been won — all we need is to live it out. When we stare right at this supercharged issue with fresh, unfiltered eyes, a seismic shift happens. Perhaps, the light at the end of racism is in sight.

https://www.amazon.com/dp/B082D16PD5/ref=cm_sw_r_tw_dp_x_4gUmFbRFX7EQQ via @amazon

The Intersection of Faith, Migration and God's Mission: A call for the people of God in the West to engage in Mission Dei

"Our missionary brothers, sisters, sons, daughters, husbands, and wives would travel thousands of miles to share the gospel to people in faraway lands. They are willing to sacrifice all to share the love of God with these people. Times are changing. Now, God is bringing people from foreign lands right to our shores. Is this a new mission? What is His reason? Unfortunately, the present political climate and rhetoric are making it extremely difficult, if not impossible, for us to have a level-headed discussion when it comes to this topic of migration. It seems the people of God are divided on what to do as well. We have been tasked to be the light of the world. We cannot hide behind nationalistic tendencies or political correctness. We must stand up and be the light in a time of darkness. We must speak the truth in love in a time of fear. We must advocate for peace in a time of hatred."

https://www.amazon.com/dp/B083P5QCW1/ref=cm_sw_r_tw_dp_x_8lUmFbYSP3NR4 via @amazon

Phones, Electronic Devices, and You: Who Is in Charge?

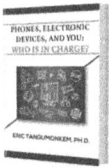

Do you have a serious fear of missing out (FOMO) when you're not online?•Do you have separation anxiety when you don't have your phone with you?•Do you text while driving? •Are your electronic devices on 24/7? If you or someone you know experience these things, read on. It is true that our phones and electronic devices have become part-and-parcel of our lives. It is connecting us in ways unimaginable. Unfortunately, it is also causing a lot of havoc in our relationships because one cannot have meaningful connections with somebody and be on the phone at the same time. This book was written to help you put your phone and electronic devices in the right place, especially when it comes to your interactions with other people. Your world will not crumble if you go offline at the appropriate times. Whose life and relationships are at stake? Yours. Take charge.

https://www.amazon.com/dp/B083P4YHRR/ref=cm_sw_r_tw_dp_x_VmUmFbT4TYCD5 via @amazon

How to Inspire Your Online student: 7 Steps to Achieving Unparalleled Success in An E-Learning Environment

Online teaching and learning are here to stay. We are living in an exciting time, with the opportunity to educate the world at our fingertips. This book makes a case for the need to bring inspiration in the online learning environment, and it explores how far this can go to raise a new generation of students who will have a local and global impact.

The flexibility, versatility, and dynamic nature of online learning holds the key to arriving at global solutions that have a regional signature. While students from all over the world are connected to world-class professors from around the globe, they will be able to receive customized solutions to meet the needs of their individual communities.

While some countries can afford the rising costs of education, others cannot. Even the countries that can afford to educate their citizens are experiencing ever-increasing expenses; one way to cut those costs without compromising quality is through online delivery.

This book explains why and how this is possible and how you, as an online instructor, can play a vital role.

https://www.amazon.com/dp/B08G5BY56D/ref=cm_sw_r_tw_dp_x_y7.qFbTME9W4Q via @amazon

How to succeed as an online student: 7 Secrets to excelling as an online student

How do you know if you have what it takes to study and succeed online? From what I have observed, there is a large chasm between "knowing" and "doing." If knowing was all that was necessary to be successful, all of us would be hugely successful. Fortunately, this book is designed in such a way that it will move you from knowing to doing. Therefore, you should make up your mind to act on the information presented in this book. Without a concerted effort to apply this information, the secrets will not work. The challenge for you might be making the necessary changes to be successful. I hope that this resource will help you succeed in your online courses.

https://www.amazon.com/dp/B08G5BY56D/ref=cm_sw_r_tw_dp_x_qE9vFbXB0ZKAQ via @amazon

To Exercise or Not to Exercise: The Connection Between Bodily Exercise and Spirituality

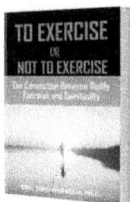

"I was given a job and given a horse to get the job done. I overworked my horse; it died, and now I cannot do my job."
This is a story that has influenced me profoundly and spurred this book.
Your body is the horse. Are you taking good care of it? Now is the best time to look after your health; your productivity depends on it.

What is the one thing that will negatively impact your productivity? No matter how talented you are and how lofty your goals, without good health, nothing else matters. While many take their health for granted and assume, they can afford to neglect it, the fact is that they cannot. The cost of ill health is so high, none of us can afford it.

This book presents a holistic approach to health, wealth, and fitness; the physical and spiritual must be in synergy for real, lasting, and sustainable success.

What's in Your Glass? Pentecostal Christians, and the Hidden Dangers of Sugary Drinks

Was the wine made by Jesus equivalent to soda pop?

Is it a sin to consume sugar-loaded drinks?

How can something sweet be bad for your health?

These and many other questions will be addressed in this book.

Most fervent Pentecostal believers do not touch any alcohol. Instead, they focus on being filled with the Holy Spirit; they take this matter seriously and do not compromise. This belief has led many to consume sugary drinks as an alternative to alcohol. There is an assumption that, since these drinks are non-alcoholic, they are safe to consume. In reality, this practice is potentially more problematic.

This book takes an in-depth look into scripture and proposes a possible solution to this sugar crisis.

IEM PRESS

To order additional copies of this book call:
214-908-3963
Or visit our website at
www.iempublishing.com

If you enjoyed this quality custom-published book
Drop by our website for more books and information

"Inspiring, equipping and motivating one author at a time."

www.ingramcontent.com/pod-product-compliance
Lightning Source LLC
Chambersburg PA
CBHW071532040426
42452CB00008B/990